GARDENING WITH THE EXPERTS

WRITTEN AND COMPILED BY

RACHEL DE THAME AND PHIL MCCANN

Published in association with the
Royal Horticultural Society

This book is published to accompany the television series entitled
Gardening with the Experts, first broadcast on BBC2 in 2003.
Series Producer: Richard Sinclair
Executive Producer: Owen Gay

ISBN 0 563 48716 X

Commissioning editor: Vivien Bowler
Project editor: Helena Caldon
Editor: Andi Clevely
Designer: Isobel Gillan
Picture researcher: Rachel Jordan
Artist: Will Giles
Production Controller: Belinda Rapley
Jacket Art Direction: Pene Parker

For more information about this and other BBC books, please visit our
website on www.bbcshop.com

Set in Sabon and Akzidenz
Printed and bound in France by Imprimerie Pollina s.a-L87954
Colour separations by Kestrel Digital Colour, Chelmsford

PAGE 2: The dry garden at RHS Hyde Hall
PAGE 3: *Aquilegia* 'Nora Barlow'
PAGE 7: The square garden at RHS Garden Rosemoor

ACKNOWLEDGEMENTS

Our thanks first and foremost to all at the Royal Horticultural Society, and in
particular the curators: Christopher Bailes, Jim Gardiner, Andrew Hart and
Matthew Wilson and their exceptional teams of dedicated gardeners.

For bringing the work of the RHS to the wider public Rachel would
particularly like to thank Jane Root and Nicola Moody. The production team
at the BBC was expertly guided by Owen Gay, with thanks also due to
series producer Richard Sinclair, and directors Neil Baldock and Mick Foley
for making the filming process so enjoyable.

At BBC Worldwide we would like to thank Robin Wood, Viv Bowler,
Helena Caldon, Pene Parker and Rachel Jordan, for their tireless efforts and
support while bringing this book to fruition.

Thanks too to Andi Clevely for his invaluable editorship, Isobel Gillan for
making the book look so good and Will Giles for producing the exquisite
illustrations.

In addition, Rachel would like to thank Phil for his extraordinary capacity
for hard work, and unique ability to retain a sense of humour while under
pressure. Grateful thanks also to Annie Sweetbaum and Hilary Murray Watts
at Arlington Enterprises and Luigi Bonomi at Sheil Land Associates Ltd for
their commitment and friendship, and to Gerard, Lauren, Joe and the rest of
the family for being there.

CONTENTS

FOREWORD

AT THE ROYAL HORTICULTURAL SOCIETY we are always looking for ways of sharing the knowledge and expertise of our gardeners. I think that they are sometimes the unsung heroes of the Society, so I have particular pleasure in introducing this book which goes some way towards paying tribute to their skills. The book accompanies a television series that is part of a dynamic association between the RHS and the BBC to extend the reach and appeal of gardening to all those with an interest in the subject.

Anyone who has visited the family of RHS Gardens – at Wisley in Surrey, Rosemoor in Devon, Hyde Hall in Essex and Harlow Carr in Yorkshire – will have seen for themselves how the dedication of the gardening staff and students not only fulfils the RHS mission to inspire, inform and educate but also, I must add, gives visitors a thoroughly enjoyable day out.

The Gardens themselves are a great inspiration, glorious to look at and full of ideas. Especially popular at Wisley are the model gardens, designed very much with the home gardener in mind. Here planting schemes can be seen, sometimes in conjunction with small trials – for instance of summer bedding schemes, vegetables in containers and fruit trees growing in small areas and trained in different styles. Elsewhere are larger-scale plantings but in many varied situations demonstrating a huge range of plants and their requirements. At Hyde Hall there is a particular emphasis on biodiversity and the dry garden is an innovative showcase for plants tolerant of drought and exposure. Rosemoor is renowned for its roses, and the series of individual outdoor 'rooms', each planted in a different style. The streamside garden at Harlow Carr is one of the most extensive in the country, and together with associated woodlands and wildflower meadows it is a rich and varied habitat for wildlife and for visitors to explore.

To help and advise our members and other visitors each Garden runs a programme of events. This includes seasonal garden walks, lectures, workshops on topics as varied as willow weaving, renovating old trees and propagation, and demonstrations. The demonstrations deal with topics that often perplex garden owners, but to see one of our gardeners or supervisory staff prune a rose or vine, or explain how to maintain a lawn or mixed border makes the operation much easier to understand. The Masterclasses in this book will give you a flavour of these demonstrations as several of our skilled gardeners and curators chat about their specialities and give tips and advice on topics such as pruning clematis, training fruit trees and planning a pond.

Our four gardens are set in very different localities and each has had its own set of problems to overcome: soil that is too light, too acid or too heavy, a lack of shelter, or a lack of moisture – to give just a few examples. In every case our gardeners have understood these problems and worked with the conditions. By caring for the soil, improving the shelter, thoughtful plant selection and expert aftercare they have created places of beauty. By following their advice in this book – and on your television screens – I hope you will be able to do the same.

Andrew Colquhoun *Director General*
ROYAL HORTICULTURAL SOCIETY

ROSES

'Roses add scent, colour and form to gardens.
In fact, they make a garden special.'

THE ROSE HOLDS A SPECIAL place in our hearts, and is unquestionably Britain's best-loved flower. Conjuring up connotations of romance and patriotism, roses are irrevocably linked with a sentimental vision of English garden style. There is a rose for every situation, ranging in scale from low-growing container-friendly varieties, to vigorous climbers capable of romping several metres through a tree. Though incredibly beautiful when grown well, roses are notoriously susceptible to a range of pests and diseases, and require pruning and deadheading to give their best.

Rosemoor, the Royal Horticultural Society Garden in Devon, is blessed with a name that suggests a rose-filled garden, and visitors would be sorely disappointed to find them absent. However, this westerly county is plagued with some of the wettest weather in the British Isles – conditions that have traditionally been considered anathema to rose-growing. Undeterred, the team of gardeners have honed their techniques to perfection, and dispelled this particular myth by growing some of the most stunning roses in the country. They have acquired a wealth of know-how which proves that the key to success is found, not in geographical locality, but in getting the cultural conditions right and selecting the best variety for each position. Now we can plunder that knowledge and apply it to our own gardens. Versatility, richness of scent and exquisitely-shaped flowers in a plethora of colours earn the rose a complete chapter in this book and, I hope, a place in your garden.

LEFT: The Cottage Garden at RHS Rosemoor; standard roses 'The Fairy', 'Bonica' and 'Iceberg' underplanted with *Lychnis coronaria*, *Eryingium alpinum*, and *Perovskia*. ABOVE: Rosa 'Graham Thomas'.

In spring check all newly-planted roses are still firm, because

wind and frost can loosen them in the soil, leading to poor growth.

If this happens, firm plants back in to the ground with your foot.

The perfect soil in which to grow great roses is a slightly acidic medium loam, neither very heavy nor too light, and packed with organic matter and fertility. Of course, few of us have these ideal conditions, but, as we see at Rosemoor, fortunately the majority of roses can tolerate a wide range of soil types.

Roses are relatively drought-tolerant but, in the other extreme, none will survive in waterlogged conditions. Very dry conditions or prolonged lack of water will impair their flowering quality and season. Soaking them with 9 litres (2 gallons) of saved rainwater during the evening will keep them going all week in a dry spell. Waterlogged soil can cause several serious root and stem problems. If your ground lies wet or boggy, especially with puddles lingering on the surface after heavy rain, you will need to improve its drainage. Very often, breaking up the soil at the bottom of planting holes with a garden fork will be enough to prevent water from sitting at the roots. On very heavy wet soils a better long-term solution is to create raised beds for roses, using plenty of rubble or similar coarse material at their base to keep the roots above the level of poor drainage.

A common fallacy is the belief that the soil must contain clay before a rose will grow well. In fact light soils can support superb rose growth if bolstered with plenty of moisture-retentive organic materials, and there are even some roses, such as many species and almost all *R. rugosa* cultivars, which thrive in light sandy conditions in preference to the heavier kinds of clay. Both extremes benefit from the addition of bulky organic matter such as well-rotted horse manure, which can fortify light soils and open up dense

heavy ground. Adding this at planting time, with further applications as a mulch every year, will go a long way towards ensuring vigorous growth.

Alkaline soils – those high in lime – can pose difficulties for roses because many essential nutrients are chemically locked into the soil, hindering or completely blocking their availability to the plants, and resulting in weak, lacklustre growth. Check the pH of the planting site with one of the readily available test kits, and compare your readings with the results chart. If your soil comes out somewhere in the range pH 6.0–7.0, the plants should be happy. Otherwise, follow the supplied instructions for raising or lowering the acidity/alkalinity levels.

In addition to their high pH status, very chalky soils may be a problem because they tend to be shallow, with just a thin layer of relatively infertile topsoil lying above a rocky subsoil of chalk layers. To grow well, a rose needs to be able to root freely in about 45–60cm (18–24in) of fertile soil – any less and it may run out of energy later in the growing season, especially in a hot dry summer. If you garden on this kind of soil, dig a sample planting hole and measure the depth of the topsoil, which is the darker friable layer lying above the chalk. Where this is insufficient, you can buy in topsoil to increase the depth over the whole area, or use topsoil or a special planting mixture for refilling each hole at planting time. Some roses are more chalk-tolerant than others, and if you combine soil improvement with growing Alba, Damask and Hybrid Musk varieties, you should meet with success.

In any soil, you can help yourself to produce top quality blooms by feeding your roses in late winter

or early spring with a specially formulated rose fertilizer. Repeat this feeding at midsummer to keep the display going into the autumn. Removing faded blooms from roses will also encourage more flowers to appear, as well as keeping the plants looking tidy; but do not deadhead if you want rose hips to develop in the autumn.

Rose sickness

This is a disabling physiological condition which can occur wherever you replace old roses with new – especially in ground where roses have been grown for many years. Properly known as rose replant disease, this results in feeble stunted topgrowth and blackened roots. Although they can sometimes recover, the new roses more usually succumb to other diseases while in this debilitated condition. The cause of the sickness is still a mystery, but it is thought that a combination of factors are involved, including soil fungi, virus-

Roses 'Erfurt', 'Bleu Magenta' and 'Goldfinch' create a stunning display in the Rose garden at RHS Garden Rosemoor.

carrying nematodes – microscopic worms that live on and around the roots – and simple nutrient depletion after years of previous rose growth.

The condition does not affect roses introduced to ground where the plants have never previously been grown, but if you are replacing old roses (or planting roses where a close relative, such as apples or cherries, used to grow), you need to take precautions. It is sometimes possible to sterilize the ground, but the safest approach is to change the soil by digging out the planting site 45cm (18in) deep over an area about 60cm (24in) across. Refill the hole with fresh topsoil from another part of the garden where roses have never grown, and add plenty of organic matter to give the new plants a strong start. The excavated soil can safely be used for other plants elsewhere in the garden.

Roses in containers

Roses are ideal plants for growing in containers, which allows you to enjoy their colour and fragrance in situations where the soil is unsuitable or where there is no open ground at all. The containers need to be large enough to support healthy growth – their depth is more critical to success than the material from which they are made. The minimum you should allow is 30cm (12in) for Miniature varieties, increasing to 45cm (18in) if you are growing Bush and Floribunda roses; vigorous Climbers, Ramblers and Shrub roses will need large tubs or half-barrels.

Line the bottom of the container with plenty of broken terracotta pot or polystyrene chunks to ensure good drainage, and then fill with fresh soil-based compost, which is more efficient than soil-less mixtures at maintaining moisture levels in summer, while its greater weight also ensures stability.

Watering is the key to successful rose growing in containers, with plants requiring water whenever the compost begins to dry out – do not rely on rainfall alone as the plant's leaf canopy often prevents it from reaching the compost. A spring and midsummer feed with a specially formulated rose food will keep plants flourishing, while larger containers benefit from a spring topdressing. Replace the top 5cm (2in) of old soil with a fresh supply, preferably mixed with a generous amount of garden compost or well-rotted manure.

Smaller-scale roses, like the Flower Carpet rose, look stunning in containers.

Choosing roses

Perhaps the most difficult and bewildering part of gardening with roses is selecting the best varieties from the hundreds that are available, supplemented annually with many more introductions. There are several main groups of roses, depending how they are classified, and two of the largest are the Hybrid Teas and Floribundas, which is where many gardeners start their collections.

Hybrid Tea roses
HTs or Large-flowered roses, as they are often called, have long slender stems, each crowned by a small cluster of shapely blooms or just a single

Iceberg produces a mass of pure white, clustered flowers.

flower, although there may be other smaller buds at its side waiting to open. They are upright and rigid in habit, generally ranging in height between 60 and 120cm (2–4ft), and bloom in flushes from early summer until late autumn, with a main display around mid- to late summer. Often regarded as the classic rose for grouping in a special bed, there are many wonderful varieties available.

Peace is a particular favourite, with large, single
  flowers made up of pale or dark yellow petals
  that are edged with pink.
Golden Jubilee has very large yellow flowers,
  tinged with pink and maturing to a rich gold,
  and is quite disease-resistant.
'Prima Ballerina' is vigorous and strikingly
  fragrant, with gorgeous buds and elegant cherry
  pink blooms.
Piccadilly, one of the earliest to flower, is vivid red
  with a yellow reverse, producing a rich bi-
  coloured effect, especially as blooms fade.

Floribunda roses

More relaxed in appearance than HTs, Floribundas produce small flowers in large heads or trusses, with a mixture of open blooms and closed buds in each cluster – indeed, they are sometimes called Cluster-flowered roses. Although rarely as shapely or fragrant as HTs, they often flower continuously throughout the summer, and with so many blooms in each cluster, plants often have a more colourful impact.

'Glenfiddich' produces gorgeous golden-amber or
  whiskey-coloured blooms over a long season,
  and its outstanding vigour ensure its popularity
  – especially in colder gardens.
Iceberg is the most popular white Floribunda,
  which looks best if allowed to grow tall and
  bushy.
Golden Wedding has clear yellow blooms, large
  and well-formed, and good disease-resistance.
'Orange Sensation' is quite startling, its large
  trusses of fragrant orange-vermilion blooms are
  guaranteed to catch the eye.

If left unsupported, Rambler roses will grow happily as ground-cover plants. Spread out their stems evenly and encourage a horizontal growth habit by pegging them in place with bent pieces of wire – metal coat hangers are good for this.

Ground-cover roses

These varieties have branches that naturally arch or grow almost parallel to the soil surface, rooting wherever they touch the ground and eventually forming dense carpets of foliage and flowers. They require little attention and are invaluable for covering inaccessible banks and large areas of barren ground. Although tough and undemanding, they are far from plain, and some varieties are quite breathtaking in full bloom.

Rosa × jacksonii 'Max Graf' is covered in summer with clusters of single apple-scented pink blooms, on thorny stems spreading to 2.4m (8ft).

Rambler rose, 'Félicité Perpetue' fills a garden with soft perfume and a vision of creamy white.

The Flower Carpet range, available in red, white, coral, pink or yellow, produces small flowers by the trugload. Growth spreads to around 1.5m (5ft) and is generally disease-resistant, especially in Flower Carpet Coral.

Some of the County series are exceptional. Wiltshire has deep pink blooms over a phenomenally long flowering period, pink Surrey is heavily fragrant, while Suffolk has some of the best orange-red hips in autumn. Hertfordshire is neat and perfect for filling in gaps between other roses or shrubs.

Ramblers for trees

With their long pliable stems and large clusters of small flowers, Rambler roses look spectacular when allowed to scramble through trees, where in late spring and summer they can bring an otherwise dull canopy to life with their dazzling blooms and attractive foliage. They can be persuaded to start colonizing a tree by initially tying their stems to the trunk and then leaving them to meander freely into the branches. Although most flower just once a year, they do so prolifically to stunning effect.

'Albertine', 5m (16ft), is often top of the favourites list. Its young leaves are an attractive shade of red, followed in early summer by copper flower buds that burst open to reveal beautiful, fragrant, soft pink flowers.

'Bobbie James', 8m (26ft), grows with gusto, its thorny stems clambering high into large trees, which it decks in early summer with clusters of white, sweetly-scented flowers, each with a central boss of golden yellow stamens.

'Félicité Perpétue', 5m (16ft), has creamy white flowers that fill the July garden with soft perfume. In mild areas it often retains its glossy foliage for much of the winter.

'Paul's Himalayan Musk', 8m (26ft), is rampant enough to cover a house. It is stunning when laden with its slightly fragrant and long-lasting blush pink blooms.

'Rambling Rector', 8m (26ft), is vigorous and floriferous, completely smothering the host tree with large clusters of white, highly fragrant flowers which fade to cream and then give way to a brilliant display of hips.

'Veilchenblau', 5m (16ft), has remarkable rich violet-mauve blooms that fade subtly to grey and produce a magical perfume of fresh apples.

Climbers for fences

With their larger flowers and more robust stems, Climbing roses need more help with support than Ramblers. They are popular for their fragrance, shapely good looks and low maintenance needs, and are a sound choice for covering walls, fences and pergolas. Most climbers are 'sports' of Hybrid Teas (a gardening synonym for a natural variation that has been isolated by propagation and grown on as a new variety) and as such share their aristocratic appearance and – in modern varieties at least – repeat-flowering habit. However, many older kinds are more like Ramblers, and bloom with a single, flamboyant early or midsummer display.

'Compassion', 3m (10ft), a popular large-flowered climber with fragrant, apricot pink flowers, branches well, making it the ideal choice for a pillar or pergola.

'Paul's Himalayan Musk' is a strong-growing rambler rose capable of covering a house or garden building.

'Danse du Feu', 3m (10ft), produces vivid orange-red blooms in clusters from midsummer into autumn and has beautiful foliage, emerging copper and turning green throughout the season.

Nice Day, 2m (6ft), is dainty and perfect for growing up supports in large containers. The blooms are salmon pink, heavily-scented and borne from tip to soil level.

Pruning roses

Phil Scott is Supervisor in the Decorative and Nursery Department at RHS Garden Rosemoor. He has been there for almost a decade and takes great pride in maintaining and planning the rose displays.

Pruning roses fills many gardeners with apprehension. Cutting away live healthy growth seems to go against every instinct to nurture and care for plants, and watch them grow. But you are actually giving them a helping hand, for if you leave plants to their own devices they will continue to put on growth, which sometimes diverts energy away from maximum flowering – our reason for planting them in the first place. Pruning can strike a happy balance between growth and flowering, as well as keeping plants vigorous and rejuvenated.

How to prune a climbing rose

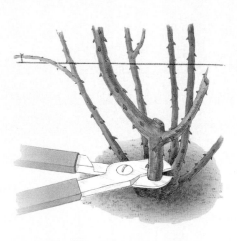

1 Completely cut out all dead or diseased branches growing from below soil level. Remove branches that cannot be trained or tied into position, and any that rub against a neighbouring branch or congest the centre of the plant.

2 If your rose is vigorous and flowers once a year, usually in the height of summer, tie the main shoots to horizontal supports and prune sideshoots to leave 10cm (4in) of growth.

3 If your variety flowers more than once a year, one in every four branches needs to be pruned to within 15cm (6in) of soil level, leaving the remaining three in four untouched.

Phil believes that 'roses add scent, colour and form to gardens. In fact, they make a garden special', and this is certainly true at Rosemoor, where the roses are some of the best in the country. The displays there form the backbone of many features within the gardens, and also combine beautifully with a wide range of perennials, grasses and shrubs.

Rather than just following the rulebook when pruning roses, Phil takes great care to look at each rose as an individual, studying its shape and direction of growth throughout the growing season. This helps considerably when he comes to prune it later in the year. So in this masterclass he shares his pruning expertise and experience.

The importance of pruning in rose cultivation

It removes dead and diseased branches.

It takes out suckers growing from the rootstock that would otherwise ruin the display or even swamp the chosen variety.

It cuts out branches that are rubbing against their neighbours, decreasing the likelihood of damage.

It removes branches from the centre of rose plants, increasing air circulation and reducing the risk of disease.

It thins out older wood and stimulates the rose to make fresh growth, which in turn produces better flowers.

The shrub rose garden at RHS Rosemoor is a spectacular sight in summer.

It is hard to kill roses with over-enthusiastic secateurs.
At worst, you may have fewer flowers, but you are more likely
to fill the garden with blooms.

RHS KNOW-HOW

- After pruning, clear up any fallen rose leaves and trimmings, as these may carry diseases into next year. Then lightly fork over the soil to loosen any compacted footprints and avoid the danger of waterlogging.

- After spring pruning, give roses a feed with a general fertilizer to boost their growth.

- Do not prune if a severe frost is forecast as this can damage open wounds, allowing diseases to enter and gain a hold.

- Equip yourself with strong thorn-proof gloves, sharp secateurs and a pruning saw if the plants are old, gnarled and in need of drastic pruning.

- Mulch round roses in spring, using a mixture of equal parts farmyard manure and finely composted bark. This acts as a protective blanket over roots, and also as a weed suppressant.

- Fish, blood and bone is an excellent organic fertilizer for using on roses in spring as growth starts. Sprinkle the recommended amount around the plants and nutrients will be released in spring, just in time for the active roots.

- Before you start pruning, always check that your secateurs are sharp and clean. This reduces the chance of leaving ragged or torn cuts at the ends of branches, which can fall victim to an infection that can then be spread by dirty secateurs.

Frequently asked questions

Why prune?

Although plants grow perfectly well in the wild without any intervention on our part, they seldom flower as lavishly as we would expect. Many plants that we grow in a domestic situation are hybrids and varieties that do not – and often could not – exist outside the garden, and so therefore they require regular attention from us to produce their best. Most would flower sparsely, for example, or succumb to disease in the free-for-all beyond our boundaries.

When is the best time to prune?

You can prune your roses in autumn or early spring, both of them times of the year when the plants are dormant and therefore will not experience a check in growth. It is a good idea to reduce the growth of large modern roses by one-third in November, which will prevent wind damage over the autumn and winter, and then complete detailed pruning of the plant in spring.

How often should a rose be pruned?

Although major pruning should be done once a year to maintain the general health, vigour and shape of a rose plant, frequent deadheading during the summer months to prolong the display is a kind of supplementary pruning.

Where on the stem do you prune?

Always look for an outward-facing bud, which will look like a small mark or raised area where a leaf once joined the stem. Cut just above this bud, making sure the cut slopes away and is not horizontal – as this stops any rainwater from running into the bud and causing damage to the plant. Being outward-facing, the bud will then grow into a shoot away from the centre of the plant, ensuring good air circulation around the stems.

Prune in spring if you want the full benefit of superb autumn hips on roses such as *Rosa moyesii* 'Geranium'.

How to prune a shrub rose

Pruning a shrub rose (illustrated here) is a similar technique to pruning a bush rose during which process you should follow step one below, and then shorten all the remaining healthy, evenly-spaced stems to within 15cm (6in) of soil level.

1 Cut out dead or diseased branches growing from below soil level, and any branches growing in the wrong direction, rubbing a neighbouring branch or overcrowding the centre of the plant.

2 Prune one shoot in four down to within 15cm (6in) of soil level, leaving the others intact if the variety flowers once annually.

3 If the shrub flowers more than once a year, prune the remaining branches to around one-third of their height.

Thornless roses

A few rose varieties are thornless and so make good choices for confined places or where they are accessible to small children. They are a pleasure to handle, but still deserve respect because the occasional spine may occur, especially after a stressful growing season.

'Zéphirine Drouhin', 3m (10ft), is perhaps the best known of these varieties. A popular Climber, it has deep pink, highly fragrant flowers that continue to appear if you deadhead regularly.

'Zéphirine Drouhin' is a fragrant favourite with gardeners who prefer thornless roses.

'Morlettii', a 2.5m (8ft) high Shrub rose, has arching growth and a single flush of magnificent magenta pink blooms. It is sometimes classed as a Boursault rose, a small group that includes other thornless varieties, such as 'Blush Boursault' and the crimson-purple climber 'Amadis'.

'François Juranville', 6m (20ft), produces a mass of mainly thornless rambling branches and cheerfully dishevelled, rosy salmon flowers, which are delightfully apple-scented.

Disease-resistant roses

Like all plants, roses are susceptible to various diseases, especially if they are grown in less than ideal circumstances. The main culprits are mildew, rust and blackspot, all of which can be controlled to a certain extent by cultural methods. Some rose varieties are known to be resistant to these diseases under normal conditions, and it is worth considering these if you are an organic gardener or prefer not to spray roses more than necessary.

'English Miss' is a lovely Floribunda with outstanding disease- and weather-resistance. It produces large sprays of camellia-shaped, blush pink blooms with a strong perfume, and at 1m (3ft) high and wide it is a strong candidate for growing in containers. Another compact Floribunda is Sexy Rexy, 1m (3ft), with clusters of highly fragrant, soft pink blooms.

'Scabrosa', 2m (6ft), is a robust Shrub rose producing large, single 13cm (5in) blooms that are rich crimson, tinged with violet and followed in autumn by large, orange-red hips.

Graham Thomas, 1.2m (4ft), is a stunning member of the English Roses group of Shrub roses, bred to combine disease resistance and repeat flowering with the beauty of old roses. Its cup-shaped blooms are rich yellow, with a fine Tea-rose fragrance. The Mayflower, 2m (6ft), is another English Rose, with rich pink blooms, while Spirit of Freedom, 2m (6ft), is a new variety, with glowing soft pink flowers that mature lilac-pink.

'Just Joey', 1m (3ft), is an elegant Hybrid Tea, with plenty of wavy, coppery-orange blooms, an enticing perfume and a long life as a cut flower. Simply Heaven, 2m (6ft), which has sophisticated pale lemon flowers with a hint of amber and a superb perfume, is another excellent HT.

Penny Lane, 4m (12ft), is a relaxed repeat-flowering Climber with good fragrance and a subtle champagne colouring. 'Compassion' (see Climbers for fences, p15) is particularly disease-resistant – just one of its many good qualities.

Roses for cut flowers

Many gardeners grow roses both for outdoor colour and for indoor display as cut flowers. They are easy to prepare for vases, provided you follow a few simple rules. Gather blooms early in the morning or evening so that stems are full of water and the plants are free from any stress caused by hot sunshine. Cut the stems just above a leaf joint and bud, making sure you do not remove more than one-third of the total length of the plant's stem.

Trim the end of the gathered stem to a sharp angle – this exposes a large amount of water-absorbent tissue, contributing to longer life in the vase. Immediately afterwards, plunge the trimmed roses in a bucket of water and leave for 12 hours to allow the stems to soak up as much water as possible. Before arranging the blooms, remove all the thorns and leaves that would otherwise be submerged, and add cut-flower fertilizer to the water to further extend their life. Tepid water does not shock the plant tissue.

Some varieties of roses are more successful than others as cut flowers. Among the best are rich crimson 'Cardinal de Richelieu' and *Rosa gallica* 'Versicolor', with its distinctive red-and-white striped blooms. Sunblest is a good yellow variety, while Margaret Merril is a fragrant blush-pink, almost white Floribunda renowned for its long life.

Buying and planting roses

Depending whether you buy from a garden centre, local nursery or a more distant mail order source, you will find that roses are grown and supplied in one of four main ways, each with its own virtues and disadvantages.

Container-grown roses have been grown in their pots for at least a year and will have developed a strong root system throughout the compost – roots can often be seen through the drainage holes in the base of the pots. This is a convenient way to buy plants and they are available all the year round, so you can plant them whenever you have time and the conditions are right. The choice is sometimes limited to the most popular varieties, although an expanding range is available in larger stores.

Bare-root roses are dug up from nursery fields, and then despatched with the minimum of soil and packaging to keep the weight down. The choice is usually extensive, particularly from

found at bargain prices. The main danger is that plants are sometimes forced into unseasonal growth in the warm, humid confines of the plastic, resulting in pale buds and stems unnaturally drawn in their search for natural light: these are unlikely to survive after planting.

Containerized roses are bare-root plants transferred to pots and packed with compost. Widely sold in many garden centres during the autumn, these do not have an extensive root system throughout the compost – you can check this by tapping the plant from its pot, when the compost will fall away leaving the roots exposed. The advantage of this method is that outlets can sell bare-root roses at container-grown prices, and if any are left unsold, they continue to develop and extend new roots, and can then be re-classed as container-grown.

Whichever type you choose, inspect the plant closely. Make sure it has a minimum of 2–3 strong stems, each at least as thick as a pencil. When buying during autumn or winter, none of the buds should show signs of growth, which would otherwise suggest the plant has been kept in warm conditions and will suffer when planted out. Stems should be well ripened – you can test this by squeezing a stem between your fingers to see if it is soft, an indication that it may have been produced late in the season and could be damaged by frost.

specialist nurseries which have the resources to grow a few examples of a wide range of varieties. Plants are lifted in the autumn once they are dormant and leafless, and must be planted out, permanently or in temporary quarters, soon after arrival and always before early spring, when buds and roots start to grow again.

Root-wrapped roses are available from many garden centres, supermarkets and even petrol stations. These are bare-root plants with a handful of compost or moss wrapped round their roots just before being enclosed in a plastic bag. The advantage of this system is that the plants are usually cheap, and – provided they are still in good condition – popular varieties can often be

Training stems horizontally checks upward growth and stimulates more flowers to develop, so arrange the stems of Ramblers and Climbers as fans on walls and twine them around pillars rather than tying them in vertically.

Heeling in

Roses bought in containers can be left undisturbed until planting conditions are right. Bare-root and root-wrapped roses may be stored for about ten days in a cool but frost-free garage or shed, after which they will need to be temporarily planted ('heeled in') to prevent the roots from drying out if permanent planting is delayed further.

To heel in roses, choose a patch of empty soil and make a shallow trench by plunging a spade into the ground and pushing it back and forth. Line the plants in the trench, spreading out their roots to make sure they are all covered, with the lowest 8cm (3in) of the stem below soil level. Push the soil back into the trench, and firm it all round the roots with your heel. This will provide adequate protection until you are ready to plant the roses in the open ground.

Permanent planting

Bare-root and container-grown roses are planted in slightly different ways.

Bare root roses: The main concern when planting one of these is to ensure that all its roots are spread out on a bed of soil, so the plant is not left suspended above a pocket of air, which can easily occur when trying to manipulate the tough inflexible roots.

Dig a planting hole 20cm (8in) deep and wide enough to take the full spread of the roots – on average, this means about 60cm (24in) across. Gently mound the soil in the centre, place the rose on top, and spread its roots outwards and down into the hole. Cover the roots with a spadeful or two of a planting mixture, made by blending together equal amounts of garden soil and either multipurpose or home-made compost. Work this around the roots with your fingers or gently shake the plant to help settle the soil. Add more planting mix, shake the plant once more and firm the mixture around the roots. Finally, refill to surface level, making sure the swollen junction between the rootstock and the topgrowth is just below the surface. Firm all round with your boot, and water the plant well.

Container-grown roses: Planting a container-grown rose is different because its roots should not be disturbed, and the most important consideration is to keep the rootball intact. Dig a planting hole 10cm (4in) larger than the container in which the rose is growing. Spread a layer of planting mixture in the base of the hole and centre the rose, still in its container, on this layer – the top of the container and the surrounding soil should be at the same level. Either cut down the side of the pot to ease out the rootball or carefully knock out the plant, and stand it in place in the hole. Gradually refill around the rootball with a blend of excavated soil and planting mixture, firming this with your hands as you go. Water the rose well, and if necessary top up with planting mixture once the soil has settled.

If you are planting Climbing roses, remember to plant them at least 45cm (18in) away from a wall, and hence away from the soil which is always drier when close to a wall and its foundations, and slope their roots away from the wall to encourage them to grow out into the open ground.

Graham Thomas grows happily when trained against a wall, flowering more profusely when branches are tied in horizontally. Catmint (*Nepeta*) adds interest to an otherwise bare base.

Clearing perennial weeds should be part of your soil preparation for planting any plants, but it is particularly impotant for Ground-cover roses; it can be difficult – and painful – if you later try to remove weeds from between a mass of mature thorny stems.

Moving roses

You can move established roses successfully during autumn, winter or early spring – at any other time of the year plants will be in active growth and resent being disturbed.

Start by preparing the new planting site. Fork over the ground thoroughly and then dig out a hole at least 60cm (24in) across and about 30cm (12in) deep, enough to accommodate the established root system. Tidy up the plant by removing any old flowers and leaves, and shorten wayward branches, especially any close to the ground – this makes it easier to dig round the main stem and reduces the chances of wind rocking the plant in its new home, loosening its roots and compromising your chances of success.

Use a sharp spade to cut all round the rose about 25cm (10in) away from its main stem. Carefully dig out the soil inside this circle to a depth of 25cm (10in), gradually loosening the roots as you go. Then dig underneath the rose at this depth until it is free. Lift the plant with its intact rootball on to a

LEFT TO RIGHT: Hips from *Rosa pimpinellifolia*, *Rosa roxburghii* f. *normalis* and *Rosa moyesii*.

hessian or plastic sheet, wrap this all round the roots and carry to the prepared planting hole. Once you have tested this is large enough, remove the sheet and ease the rootball into the hole. Fill in all round with a soil and compost mix, firming this with your hands. Finally level the soil and water the plant well, continuing this regularly in dry weather until you see signs of new growth.

Raising your own roses

Bought roses are almost always produced by grafting the chosen variety on to a rootstock of known vigour, but there are two other propagation techniques that are particularly useful for trying at home.

Growing roses from seed

This is the way rose breeders develop new varieties. It takes a few years before a seedling plant is mature enough to flower, and its blooms and habit may not match either of the parent plants. Results are very variable if you have saved seeds from hybrid roses, which are always unpredictable, unlike species roses, which usually produce identical offspring.

After cleaning seeds extracted from rose hips, float them in a dish of water. Any that sink are viable and can be sown with a chance of success, whereas the ones that float are useless and should be discarded.

Collecting the seeds is easy. Harvest the hips when they are ripe – usually in late autumn – and spread them on 2cm (1in) layer of multipurpose compost in a tall pot. Cover with a 2cm (1in) layer of compost, and then add another layer of hips, followed by more compost. Continue until the pot is full, finishing with a layer of compost. Stand the pot in a cold place in the garden to allow winter frosts to break down the germination inhibitors present in the hips.

The following spring, knock out the contents of the pot in prepared seed drills in a spare part of a border. Seedlings will soon emerge, often in flushes, and you can transplant the strongest for growing on elsewhere. With smaller quantities, cut the ripe hips open to extract the seeds, which you need to wash in clean water, and then sow them in pots or trays of multipurpose compost. Keep these in a cold frame over winter, and seedlings will appear the following spring.

Roses from cuttings

Another way to produce new plants is to take hardwood cuttings in September. This is quicker than sowing seeds, often producing a young flowering plant within a year or two, and the results are predictable because the new plant will be exactly the same as its parent.

Select a shoot as thick as a pencil from the current year's growth, making sure it is healthy, with no signs of pests, diseases or flowers. Trim it above a bud at the top and just below a bud at the lower end to leave a straight cutting about 25cm (10in) long. Remove all but the uppermost pair of leaves and break off all the thorns along the shoot, which is easy to do if the shoot is really ripe.

Dig a narrow trench 20cm (8in) deep and line the bottom with a 5cm (2in) layer of sharp sand. Push the lower end of the cutting into the sand and firm it in an upright position. Refill the trench with soil and firm round the cutting, leaving the pair of top leaves just above the soil surface. Water well and refirm. Roots will start to form within six weeks, and your new plants will be ready for lifting and transplanting in the spring, or you can leave them until the autumn if growth is slow.

Breeding new varieties

Rose breeding is simple and exciting, and could be financially rewarding if you manage to raise a new variety that can prove its worth in trials.

First, choose two parent plants, each with desirable characteristics such as colour, shape, vigour or resistance to weather or disease. In the autumn, pot them up and move them to a cool greenhouse, which should be kept well ventilated. Water and feed them from spring onwards.

They will produce flowers in May, when you can prepare them for cross-pollination. Remove the petals and anthers from a half-opened flower on the plant that is to produce the seeds, and then wrap the prepared bloom in a paper bag. Next day, choose a fully open flower on the other parent, the pollen donor, remove its petals carefully and brush the anthers against the exposed stigma of the seed parent. Replace the bag over the fertilized flower and label it with the names of both parents and the date.

About a fortnight later, you can remove the bag and allow the hips, which contain the seeds, to develop normally until ripe, when they are harvested and prepared for sowing as above.

'Perennials are an essential part of the garden, they add loads of colour and texture. You can't help but admire them.'

I F TREES AND SHRUBS FORM the backbone of a garden, then perennials and grasses are the muscles and flesh. All are plants that die down at the end of the growing season, and reappear the following spring. There are perennials suitable for all conditions, whether sun or shade, acid or alkaline and wet or dry. They form an enormous group, covering the full spectrum of flower and foliage colour, and ranging in stature from a few centimetres to a couple of metres or more in height and spread. Encompassing countless flowering plants and grasses, perennials provide the bulk of our most popular plants, and are crucial to the success of a planting scheme.

Whatever style and atmosphere one aspires to, for most of us the perfect garden would be hard to achieve without perennials and grasses, and far less fun to create. They are also among the most enjoyable plants to grow, and are generally easy to care for. However, one can never have too much good advice, and the Royal Horticultural Society gardeners responsible for maintaining the ornamental beds are a mine of information. In their care, the gardens overflow with an abundance of perennials, and at every turn swathes of glorious flowers and silky grasses take your breath away. The sheer scale of these stunning planting combinations can be overwhelming, but they are nevertheless a valuable source of inspiration and are packed with ideas that can be scaled down to your own more modest plot. I always leave an RHS garden with a list of exciting new plants to try.

LEFT: *Stipa gigantea*, *Penstemon* 'Alice Hadley' and *Lathyrus* 'Midnight' at RHS Garden Wisley.
ABOVE: *Papaver orientale* 'Patty's Plum'.

Peonies do not like being transplanted. Do not expect an offshoot transplanted from elsewhere to flower for at least three or four years – but the display will be worth waiting for.

Perennials are plants that live for more than two years. Trees and shrubs are perennials but mostly the term is used to describe herbaceous, non-woody plants that die down in winter, and which, once mature, will flower every year. They form a huge group that includes many favourite garden plants revered for their architectural beauty, shape, form and, of course, their flowers. The leaves of many perennials are also outstanding, with textures that can range from tough and glossy to silky or fragile, and colours that can rival those of their blooms.

Traditionally, herbaceous perennials have been grown in large beds, flanked by a lawn or paths and positioned at the side of the garden or as an island bed, planned to be enjoyed from all sides. The principle of growing taller perennials at the back of the bed (or in the centre of islands), with smaller plants at the front is well-established and still relevant – planting in ranks is like organizing a group photograph: all are visible and none hidden from view. Perennials can also be grown in mixed beds, combined with shrubs and other woody plants. Whichever style you choose, there are perennials that will be in flower at virtually any time of the year.

Early perennials

These offer some of the earliest colour in the garden, often coinciding with the main crop of spring bulbs.

Doronicum grandiflorum (leopard's bane) grows best in semi-shade and moist soil. 'Miss Mason' is delightful with cheerful yellow daisy-like blooms in April, and grows to 60cm (24in) tall and wide.

Doronicum orientale 'Magnificum' flowers in spring, with masses of large heads of bright yellow blooms that are wonderful for cutting. It is happiest in moist soil and partial shade or full sun, and grows 90cm (3ft) tall by 60cm (24in) wide.

Epimedium grandiflorum enjoys woodland conditions, where it can revel in dappled light and moist soil. It is a gorgeous plant, 30cm (12in) high and broad, with evergreen foliage that is finely toothed and reddish-green, and deep pink and white flowers in spring. There are many choice varieties.

Iris sibirica 'Dreaming Yellow' is a beautiful late spring perennial with branching stems bearing three or four flowers that start creamy-yellow and fade to white. Its clumps grow best in moist soil, and can reach 90cm (3ft) tall with an indefinite spread.

Paeonia mlokosewitschii is one of the earliest peonies to open. Its clear yellow blooms seem quite translucent against a cloudless spring sky. Plants grow 75cm (30in) high and wide in well-drained soil with full sun.

Symphytum × uplandicum 'Variegatum' is a variegated form of Russian comfrey, with cream and grey-green leaves. In spring blue buds open to reveal startlingly purple flowers. Happy in a sunny or partially-shaded spot where the soil does not dry out, it grows 90cm (3ft) tall by 60cm (24in) wide.

Verbena bonariensis produces a base of leaves from which wiry stems of purple flowers emerge. Plants start blooming in early summer and last until autumn. It grows 1.5m (5ft) high with a 60cm (2ft) spread.

Mid-summer perennials

The widest range, with an almost bewildering choice. Here is a selection that includes something for everyone.

Acanthus spinosus is statuesque with gleaming, spiny dark green leaves and towering 1.5m (5ft) spires of hooded flowers in white and mauve. Plants spread to 90cm (3ft), and prefer well-drained soil in sun or shade.

Agastache foeniculum 'Alabaster' (anise hyssop) is a floriferous perennial, with dense spikes of ivory-white summer flowers crowning its scented foliage. Best in full sun and well-drained soil, it grows 90cm (3ft) tall with a similar spread and may be short-lived, but readily self-seeds.

Alchemilla mollis (lady's mantle) has fresh lime-green leaves that can star in flower arrangements and hold the morning dew in their crimped centres with perfect poise. Clouds of yellowish-green flowers are produced in summer on clumps 30cm (12in) high and wide. It will thrive in almost any soil and position.

Centranthus ruber (red valerian) has fleshy grey-green stems and leaves, and pyramids of vibrant red blooms that often self-seed. Content in any soil, it grows to 90cm (3ft) high with a similar spread in rich conditions, but looks more compact in light, poor soil.

Geraniums – true hardy geraniums, or cranesbills – form the backbone of many perennial borders. They are virtually indestructible, but grow best in moisture-retentive soils with plenty of organic matter dug in at planting time. *G. wallichianum* 'Buxton's Variety' will wander happily through borders, and produces white-flecked leaves and blue flowers with white centres all summer. Plants grow 45cm (18in) tall by 90cm (3ft) wide.

Knautia macedonica bears crimson pincushion flowers on wiry stems throughout the summer. A floppy plant 90cm (3ft) tall and wide, it benefits from supporting neighbours or canes and grows best in well-drained soil in the sun.

Ligularia 'The Rocket' adds majesty to a damp shady border. Its huge leaves, dark green and toothed, wilt if the soil dries out, but quickly revive with moisture to provide a lush background to the spectacular towering spires of brilliant yellow flowers that soar 2.1m (7ft) into the summer sky. Spread 90cm (3ft).

Papaver orientale 'Patty's Plum' is a beauty, with deeply cut leaves and large purple blooms that look and feel like tissue paper, and often reach 15cm (6in) in diameter. Plants prefer well-drained soil and a sunny position, and grow 90cm (3ft) tall and wide.

Penstemons flower all summer in a multitude of colours. 'Hidcote Pink' produces soft pink tubular flowers, 'Sour Grapes' has small violet blooms with deep pink throats, and 'Schoenholzeri' is a stunning ruby scarlet; 'White Bedder' is one of the best white varieties. The black anthers in every penstemon flower lend a freckled charm to their display. Plants grow 90cm (3ft) tall and wide, and are best pruned just above ground level in spring for maximum performance.

Phlox paniculata is available in a range of cultivars that can be sumptuous, extrovert and even flamboyant in their colouring – there are white, pink, red, lilac, orange-tinted and bi-coloured, all growing well in sun or partial shade with moist but well drained soil. They form sprawling clumps that often need support from cages or canes, and grow 1.5m (5ft) with a 90cm (3ft) spread. 'Mount Fuji' produces large pure white heads, 'Brigadier' is orange, 'Aida' violet-red, and 'Bright Eyes' is pale pink with a dark eye.

Late-season perennials

These are valuable plants that spend all summer growing in size and then burst into colour late, just when you thought the season was nearly over.

Actaea pachypoda (white baneberry) always draws autumn visitors at RHS Garden Wisley. Stout scarlet stalks bear clusters of white berries (poisonous) above a yellow-green background of divided foliage in October and November. Growing to 90cm (3ft) high and 60cm (24in) wide, plants need moist, lightly shaded woodland conditions.

Anemone × hybrida varieties are vigorous and flower in early autumn in almost any situation. The simple blooms are cup-shaped, in shades of pink, white, rose or purple, and look delightful as they nod on wiry stems in the autumn sunshine. Plants grow 1.5m (5ft) high with a spread of 60cm (24in). 'Honorine Jobert' is a popular pure white variety, 'Max Vogel' a sensational contrast with semi-double mauve blooms.

Aster novae-angliae and *Aster novi-belgii* (Michaelmas daisies) are the kings and queens of the late border, flowering throughout autumn in sun or partial shade and rich well-drained soil. *A. novi-belgii* varieties are more prone to mildew than *A. novae-angliae*, although keeping the plants moist can reduce infections. Pinch out growing shoots in spring to produce bushier plants smothered in masses of blooms. Examples of the tremendous choice are *A. novi-belgii* 'Little Pink Beauty', 45cm (18in) tall, and *A. novae-angliae* 'Harrington's Pink', 1.2m (4ft), both an attractive soft pink.

Heleniums or sneezeweeds, are great for introducing bold colours in early autumn. *Helenium* 'Moerheim Beauty' is outstanding, with deep green foliage and coppery orange-red blooms. Plants grow 80cm (32in) high and spread to 60cm (24in).

Kniphofias (red-hot pokers) last well, their strong spikes of incandescent blooms lighting up the autumn sky. 'Prince Igor' is one of the tallest, 1.8m (6ft) high, with large red flowers fading to yellow at the base of the spikes. A superb smaller variety is 'Little Maid', just under 90cm (3ft), with slender foliage and yellow flowers.

All-year-round perennials

Some perennials offer evergreen foliar colour as well as a flower display, and these really earn their place in any border.

Ajuga reptans 'Atropurpurea' (bugle) is superb ground-cover, its evergreen leaves clustered into neat rosettes that spread by runners, often covering a square metre of bare soil within a couple of years. The glossy leaves of this variety are deep bronze-purple, topped in spring by spikes of richest blue flowers.

Artemisia absinthium 'Lambrook Silver' (wormwood) has masses of silvery evergreen leaves that are finely divided and highly aromatic. The bushy plants produce small flowers in summer, but these are best nipped off as they add little to the overall splendour of this beautiful perennial. Plants grow 90cm (3ft) high and 60cm (24in) wide.

Helleborus × hybridus (Lenten Rose) is one of the best all-year-round performers. The cup-shaped flowers, produced in winter and early spring over a perennial clump of divided evergreen leaves, are various shades of pink, purple or white. It is perfectly hardy in dappled light, with an occasional organic mulch, and grows 45cm (18in) high and wide.

The cottage-garden look

A true cottage-style garden is a stimulating, apparently chaotic jostle of perennials, annuals, shrubs, edibles and trees, all growing together and producing flowers for vases and food for the table. The following perennials are just a few indispensable plants which re-create that traditional informal garden style.

Acanthus spinosus against a background of Clematis 'Etoile Violette'

Aquilegias or columbines are firm cottage garden favourites. Easy to grow and available in a vast array of colours, they self-seed into every nook and cranny. *Aquilegia* 'Hensol Harebell' is an old-fashioned variety with rich blue flowers, and *A. vulgaris* 'Nora Barlow' is a double form with cream, green and red petals. Plants grow 75–90cm (30–36in) high and 60cm (24in) wide.

Dianthus include scented pinks which are another mainstay of cottage gardens with light soils and plenty of sunshine. *Dianthus* 'Mrs Sinkins' is one of the most fragrant, with slightly dishevelled white blooms with green centres. Plants grow 45cm (18in) high and 30cm (12in) wide.

Their large spikes of showy flowers made lupins a great favourite in traditional borders. *Lupinus* 'The Governor' adds blue and white to the maelstrom of cottage garden colours, and can grow 1.5m (5ft) tall. If this is too much, try the Gallery Series, only 60cm (24in) high and available in a range of colours for the front of borders or containers.

No cottage garden would look right in spring without primulas, and in particular, primroses. Well before the dense foliage of taller perennials cast too much shade, the pale yellow blooms of *Primula vulgaris* appear in charming profusion. Plants are 15cm (6in) high with a similar spread, and quietly thrive and multiply if left undisturbed.

Planting perennials

Container-grown perennials are available from good nurseries twelve months of the year, so you can plant whenever your soil permits.

Enrich the site first with plenty of compost or well-rotted manure. Dig a hole a little larger than the pot your perennial is growing in, and ease the plant from its pot. Centre its rootball in the hole, and refill all round with soil so the plant is at the correct depth. Firm around the crown of the plant and give it a good soak, then mulch.

With vigorously self-seeding perennials cut all growth back by two-thirds
after flowering. This removes the seedheads and stimulates the plants to
grow again and often produce a late second flush of blooms.

Spring is a popular time for planting, because the plants look good in garden centre displays, you can see what you are buying, and April showers will gently water them in after planting, but you will also need to water in dry weather. Autumn can be an even better time to plant, however, as the soil is warm after the summer season and usually moist from autumn rains – perennials love this and their roots will often continue to grow throughout autumn and mild spells in winter, their topgrowth bursting into life again as soon as spring arrives.

Specialist nurseries may offer perennials as bare-root plants in the autumn, giving gardeners a wider choice, often at lower prices. These plants are lifted from the nursery fields, packaged and sent out at the right time. Planting is the same as for container-grown perennials: enrich the soil beforehand with plenty of well-rotted organic matter and make sure the plant is watered well afterwards, then mulch.

Perennial care

Deadheading is vital if you want to encourage perennials to continue producing flowers. Once seed has been formed the plant has achieved its goal – to reproduce – and flower production is stopped. However, remove the flowers before the seed develops and the plant continues to flower in the vain hope of producing seed. There is a time and a space for allowing seeds to develop, and that's in a cottage garden – here you might actively encourage plants to seed, and they will do so readily. The seed is then self-sown into the soil and new seedlings appear, giving a marvellous jumbled appearance to your garden. It is astounding where

plants can self-seed; you only need an aquilegia to set seed and seedlings will appear in between concrete slabs, in tiny cracks and even on walls.

Plant adaptability

Plants are masters of adaptation, especially those capable of thriving in warm dry conditions. Water evaporates naturally from a plant's leaves by a process called transpiration, but most drought-tolerant species have evolved various modifications in order to reduce these losses. Some have developed tiny leaves which they keep close to the ground, for example, while others have large, fleshy leaves that can store up water for use in hard times.

Hairiness is another cunning strategy, because fine leaf hairs can trap any available water, such as morning dew, and channel it down to the roots where it is absorbed. A waxy coating can trap moisture within the leaf and reflect hot sunlight, as do grey or silver leaves, reducing heat and the resulting demands on the plant's water content.

Out of sight below ground, roots have adapted in two main ways. Some species produce long taproots that search for water deep in the soil and then store it in their fleshy root tissue until needed. Other plants go to the opposite extreme, producing a fine network of roots just below the surface of the soil, where they absorb any available water the moment it reaches the ground.

Propagating perennials

There are two main ways to propagate perennials – by division or by taking shoot cuttings. Both are cheap and easy methods of producing many more new plants that are identical to the original plant.

Division

This is an easy method of multiplying plants, requires no specialist tools, and if done at the right time will quickly increase stocks simply by removing rooted portions that develop naturally around the original plant once it is established. Because most perennials grow and increase in size to form large clumps, many plants benefit from lifting and dividing every three to four years. By discarding the woody, central portion of the stem, you can rejuvenate an established plant. The whole clump of the plant can be divided by first lifting it clear of the ground and then plunging two garden forks into its centre. Lever these back and forth to split the clump into two or more segments, which can be replanted in fresh well-prepared sites. Smaller portions can be obtained by slicing through the clump with a spade or sharp knife – provided the new fragment has both stem and roots, it will readily grow into a new plant identical to its parent. Small plantlets can also be pulled from the edge of a clump by hand.

Shoot cuttings

These are taken in early spring as the new shoots are bursting through the soil. Scrape soil away from the base of the plant to reveal where the shoots originate, and then sever them as close to the parent as possible. Place them in a polythene bag to prevent water loss, and take them indoors for preparation and rooting. Use a sharp knife to trim the base of each shoot just below a leaf joint – you might have to look carefully for this if the leaves are still immature and small – the finished cutting should be about 5cm (2in) long. Nip off any larger leaves, and then gently push the cuttings into a pot of multipurpose compost mixed with an equal volume of grit for enhanced drainage. Just leave the top third of each cutting exposed. Water, allow to drain and place a polythene bag over the pot, ensuring the polythene does not touch the cuttings; alternatively, use a propagator with a high lid. Check daily and water before the compost dries out, and pot up the cuttings individually when roots appear through the base of the pot.

Root cuttings

These are easy to take and the best technique with perennials such as echinops and oriental poppies – which can be difficult to lift, have fat roots and produce poor stem cutting material. The method imitates the way in which perennial weeds often revive from cut fragments of their roots. Late winter is the best time to take the cuttings, while plants are still dormant. Note that plants with variegated leaves usually produce green foliage when raised from root cuttings.

Scrape away some of the soil to expose the roots, or dig up the plant, if this is possible, and wash it free of soil. Select a root the thickness of a pencil, sever it from the parent, and then use a sharp knife to divide it into 5cm (2in) lengths. Trim these lengths diagonally at the end nearest to the original root tip and horizontally at the other end, so that you insert the cuttings the right way up.

Insert them (diagonal cut downwards) in pots of multipurpose compost mixed with an equal amount of grit, and leave the horizontally cut ends level with the surface. Cover with a further 5mm (¼in) of compost/grit mix, topped with 5mm (¼in) of pure grit. Label and stand the pot in a cold

After sowing seeds outdoors, sow a few more in pots on a windowsill.

Indoor seeds will germinate faster so it will be clear which are weeds and

which are the seedlings when the new plants appear outside.

frame or a propagator set at 10°C (50°F) until new shoots appear, when the plants can be individually potted into 9cm (3in) pots of compost/grit mixture.

Root cuttings can also be taken from perennials with thinner roots, such as phlox. Lift and trim the cuttings in the same way into 5cm (2in) segments (no need to distinguish their ends), and then lay them on the surface of a seed tray filled with the compost/grit mix. Cover with 5mm (¼in) of the mixture, label and treat as above.

Sowing seeds

This can be done in early summer, either directly outdoors or in the protection of a greenhouse. Prepare an outdoor seedbed by hoeing, raking and removing all stones, rogue roots and weeds, and then rake again until the texture is similar to breadcrumbs. Mark out a shallow drill with a bamboo cane at the depth recommended on the seed packet. Water the drill and allow to drain.

Sow seeds thinly along the length of the drill and cover with multipurpose compost, which will be a different colour and mark their position, making weeding easier. Allow seedlings to grow until they are large enough to handle, when you can transplant them into their permanent positions or 15cm (6in) apart in a nursery bed to grow on until the autumn.

Small, expensive or temperamental seeds can be sown in trays or pots in a greenhouse, cold frame or on a windowsill. Fill trays or pots with multipurpose compost and sow the seeds thinly on the surface. Cover with the recommended depth of compost and stand the tray or pot in a little water, leaving this to rise up, evenly soaking the

compost and seeds. Allow to drain and then stand on a windowsill or in a shaded part of the greenhouse. Cover with polythene bags or propagator lids to create a humid microclimate. Regularly check for water requirements and signs of the seedlings emerging – when these are large enough, they can be transplanted outdoors.

Staking perennials

Perennials, especially the tallest kinds, can sprawl languidly, sometimes damaging themselves or neighbouring plants unless staked in time. If they grow sufficiently close, you can use nearby shrubs to support perennials, but very often you will need to provide temporary support once the plant is growing strongly. The simplest method is to insert a ring of bamboo canes around the plant's perimeter, making a framework to wind garden twine or raffia around and stop the growth from collapsing.

Metal stakes with linking horizontal arms are a popular choice, and can be arranged to support any sized plant. The stakes are pushed into the soil, avoiding the area around the roots, and then linked together to form a strong framework. Shoots are supported well, and later grow over and around the stakes, hiding them and creating a natural look in your borders. Plastic or metal mesh cages can be positioned over developing plants to support their shoots, which also grow to disguise the mesh. Twiggy prunings are a home-grown option that can be pushed into the soil, making sure that the tops of the twigs are lower than the final height of the plant. Depending on the species you choose, some twigs may take root and can be transplanted at the end of the growing season.

Creating a dry garden

Matthew Wilson is Curator of the RHS Garden Hyde Hall, where he and his dedicated team have built and planted a superb dry Mediterranean garden which he calls 'A testament to the versatility of plants'.

Making a purpose-built dry garden using Mediterranean plants is just one of many options for a landscape designer, but sometimes it is the only practical way to manage challenging conditions. Imagine, for example, a site on clay soil in one of the driest parts of the United Kingdom, in a country that must import 75% of its water at peak times to cope with rising demand and falling natural supply, and then set about planning a garden that is filled with colour and interest as well as being attractive to wildlife. This is exactly what has happened at Hyde Hall in Essex.

Working in partnership with local water companies, Matthew Wilson has designed a garden which thrives without any artificial irrigation, using a range of plants that tolerate drought and exposure to drying winds, yet manage to be aesthetically pleasing. The heavy clay soil was just an extra challenge. The result is a triumph, and a showpiece of what can be done if you understand and work with the specific needs of plants.

Tips from Hyde Hall

- Allow plants to self-seed by leaving seedheads to ripen naturally, and do not use a planting membrane under any mulch as this can stop seedlings rooting directly into the soil.

- Use waste or recycled materials, such as builder's rubble or stones raked and gathered from around the garden. The rock used at Hyde Hall for their Mediterranean garden was to be crushed and used for road-building – it looks much better in this garden.
- Plant first and mulch later. This is easier than trying to plant through the protective surface layer, and can prevent gritty mulch materials from falling into planting holes.
- Plant small specimens. These adapt more readily, whereas larger plants demand more and longer care, especially watering, which defeats the whole purpose of the garden.
- Put the fertilizer away, because dry-garden plants have evolved to cope with nutrient-deficient soil and will not welcome extra feeding.
- Leave topgrowth over winter, and then cut it all down in spring. This will scatter ripe seeds around the garden and remove the dead foliage just in time for new spring growth.

Mediterranean plant combinations

The combination of *Perovskia* 'Blue Spire' and *Diascia* 'Joyce's Choice' can guarantee an eye-catching display. The perovskia's grey-white stems and aromatic leaves are remarkable on their own,

Establishing a dry garden

1 Prepare the base of the dry garden by assembling mounds of builder's rubble, and enclose these with rocks, boulders or railway sleepers.

2 Spread a layer of graded topsoil over the mounds, using a free-draining mixture such as garden soil blended with an equal volume of sandy soil. Build and shape this to the desired contours and levels.

3 Plant high, leaving half the rootball above the topsoil level, and then spread a gravel mulch around the plants and over the whole soil surface.

but from late summer well into autumn they are topped by 1.5m (5ft) spikes of violet-blue flowers. Team these with the large apricot flowers of dainty *Diascia* 'Joyce's Choice', just 30cm (12in), and you will produce a stunning partnership.

Stipa tenuissima is a deciduous perennial grass with slender light green foliage and gorgeous arching heads of fluffy flowers in early summer, lasting well into autumn when they can look breathtaking encrusted with a hard frost. By planting it near some gabbro – a pinkish igneous, glacial rock transported from Aberdeen – Matthew has achieved an enchanting combination, especially when the grass billows softly in the sunlight and summer breezes, producing a mesmerising play of shadows on the rocks.

RHS KNOW-HOW

- Never use pesticides if you want to attract wildlife; organic gardens are a great attraction for invertebrates, mammals and birds.
- Site a dry Mediterranean garden so that it faces west or south to receive the most sunlight. If arranged with an east- or north-facing aspect, many plant species could fail because they get insufficient sun.
- When mulching young plants with gravel, cover each one with an upturned plant pot so that you can spread the material more easily without the risk of damaging any delicate stems. Once you have covered the intervening ground, remove the pots and ease the gravel up to the plant stems.

Many grasses can be invasive, taking over flower borders.

so grow them in containers placed within the borders where their

beauty is concentrated – it also saves time weeding.

Grasses

A large and world-wide family of evergreen and herbaceous plants, grasses are distinguished by having growing points at the base of their leaves, which tend to be narrow and strap-like, in tufts, cushions or mats. Their flower heads, usually held high above the main plant and occurring at almost any time of the year, according to species and variety, are composed of numerous blooms gathered in globes, spikes or long plumes.

Grasses are some of the most stylish plants, and although for many gardeners they have never been out of fashion, they are only now used as key plants for garden designers. Grasses combine well with most plants, bringing colour and leaf form to plantings, and adding grace and poise to mixed borders. Grasses look spectacular when grown in drifts through beds and they also invaluably provide a resting spot for your eye when surveying a herbaceous border. The riot of colour is calmed by large clumps of grass, your eye will pause then carry on into the melee of colour, form and texture. Whether in drifts, clumps or as individuals, grasses also look at home near water. Sun playing on grass leaves quietly dipping into gently running water is one of the many pure delights of gardening.

Grasses in containers

Grasses grow well in containers and look serene when dotted as individuals on patios or in amongst beds and borders. Choose a tall pot or tub that will allow the grass to tumble gracefully down the sides and produce an elegant cascading feature. Put crocks or chunky pieces of polystyrene in the base to aid drainage and to stop any compost from being washed through the drainage holes, and then fill with well-drained compost. After planting, topdress the soil with slate chippings or gravel to ensure water does not collect round the crown of the plant, causing it to rot.

When growing any plants in containers you need to check watering requirements carefully – rainwater is often prevented from reaching the compost due to the dense canopy of leaves. So check containers every day, even after it has rained, and water whenever necessary. A sprinkle of seaweed extract in spring will feed plants for the whole of the growing season.

Ornamental grasses

There are many different and lovely grasses to choose from, some of them annuals. This is a selection of the most reliable perennial kinds.

Arundo donax (giant reed) is big, often reaching 3m (10ft) tall and 60cm (24in) wide in a single year. Its cream-striped fresh green foliage is impressive as a highlight in a perennial/grass border, especially with its summer barley-white flowers. A sunny position and moist, well-drained soil suit this eye-catching plant best.

Calamogrostis × acutiflora 'Overdam' (feather reed grass) is a stunning combination of white and green stripes with a pink flush, topped in early summer by airy grey-pink blooms. Cut back the leaves in midsummer to encourage fresh strong growth. It grows equally well in sand or clay, but it prefers semi-shade, and in the right conditions can reach 90cm (3ft) tall by 60cm (24in) wide.

Deschampsia flexuosa 'Tatra Gold' (tufted hair grass) produces clumps of golden yellow leaves, each as thin as a needle. It is indifferent to sun or shade, but the soil should never be allowed to dry out. Coppery-bronze flowers appear in June and July on plants 45cm (18in) high and 30cm (12in) wide.

Hakonechloa macra 'Aureola' starts in spring as a stunning yellow and green-striped grass, changing in summer to russet-brown with spikes of reddish-brown flowers in autumn. It is a bright accent for sun or semi-shade, in containers or moist well-drained borders. It grows 45cm (18in) high and wide, and may need winter protection in cold gardens.

Hordeum jubatum (squirreltail barley) has fairly plain foliage, but its summer blooms make a glorious highlight for sunny sites with good drainage. Arching spikes of feathery summer flowers, creamy white tinged with pink, erupt from plants that are 60cm (24in) high and 30cm (12in) wide. Cut back after flowering to prevent lavish self-seeding and to encourage a second late display. Alternatively, transplant seedlings into pots of well-drained compost, grow on and replant elsewhere in the garden to produce a breathtaking display.

The combination of *Calamagrostis* x *acutifolia* 'Overdam', *Aster amellus* 'Violet Queen', and *Miscanthus sinensis* works to stunning effect.

Imperata cylindrica 'Rubra' (Japanese blood grass) has superb foliage, lime green tipped with red while young and ageing to blood red by midsummer, but not fully hardy. Best in a sunny position and moist soil, where it slowly spreads into fat clumps, it will grow to 45cm (18in) with a similar spread.

Miscanthus sinensis 'China' (maiden grass or eulalia) is a choice plant for a sunny spot in any soil. Its dense clumps of slim olive green leaves grow to 1.5m (5ft) high; large red flower sprays appear in late summer, just before the foliage turns a rich shade of russet brown.

Molinia caerulea 'Variegata' (moor grass) forms tussocks of cream and green leaves, especially effective in moist soils against a dark background. Compact purple spikes of blooms crown buttery yellow flower stems in June. Plants grow 45cm (18in) high with a similar spread. It grows well in containers of well-drained compost.

Pennisetum alopecuroides (Chinese fountain grass) has superb foliage, narrow and mid-green, arching from plants that are 90cm (3ft) tall and 45cm (18in) wide. A fountain of tall flower stems, each tipped with a foxtail bloom with conspicuous purple bristles, erupts in late summer and lasts well into winter.

Stipa gigantea (giant feathergrass) is an impressive evergreen, with long, thin mid-green leaves growing in clumps 2.4m (8ft) tall and 90cm (3ft) wide. From midsummer until autumn it produces long spikes of silvery, white feathery blooms that dangle and dance gracefully in the breeze. A superior grass for a sunny well-drained position.

Grass care

Grasses will reward you with fantastic form and shape and look wonderful when partnered with perennials, and they are not as labour-intensive as you might think. Few pests or diseases cause serious problems for grasses.

Never firm compost around cuttings with your fingers as this may damage

them. A firm tap of the pot on the bench, followed by watering from above,

will be sufficient to ensure good root contact with the compost.

Feeding grasses

Over-fed grasses produce weak, sappy growth that can become elongated. It is far better to grow your grasses without the use of additional fertilizers. Add organic matter to planting holes and allow the soil to provide everything the grass needs. Weak, sappy growth is also susceptible to attacks from pests and diseases.

Grasses grown in containers do not have the benefit of a fertile, evolving soil, and do rely on the compost for all their needs. But, again, over-use of fertilizers will produce weak growth. For established plants, scrape away the top 2.5cm (1in) of compost and replace with fresh compost in spring. When replacing the compost check for offshoots that are formed readily around the base of the parent plant.

Cutting grasses

Some gardeners garden by the calendar, while others study their plants and garden only when the plant needs attention. Look closely at your grasses and keep an eye on the weather – the rest comes naturally.

It's best to cut ornamental grasses back when the new shoots are just appearing among the dead leaves. Then these dead leaves should be cut back to just above the tips of the new shoots. If you trim before the new shoots appear, you will run the risk of exposing the plant to severe weather. If you prune when the new shoots start to elongate, you can accidentally cut them or leave too much dead growth and the whole effect is poor. Spring cut back can be made as late as mid March in some colder areas. It's also a great excuse to wander around your garden every day of the year.

However, it also pays dividends to leave old leaves and flower heads on ornamental grasses throughout the winter. The old growth protects the crown of the plant and therefore the area where new shoots are destined to appear the following spring. Old, dead growth and flower heads on plants can also look sensational – frosted seed heads are a joy in the winter garden, especially when illuminated by the low, weak winter sun. Birds too enjoy the last few seeds remaining in the seed heads.

Take care when cutting out the old growth as it is dry, and so dry that a spark, a match or any naked flame can ignite the stems so that whole plants can quickly become a fire hazard.

Propagation

Large plants will develop several growing heads. This produces a bushy clump of grass that looks attractive, but it is also premier division material and as such will provide many more plants for free. To divide the plant, ease it out from its position – the ground or its container – and place it on a potting bench. Tease away the soil from around the developing main heads, and then either pull the heads apart, ensuring each has a large section of root attached, or cut with a sharp knife. Always include the leaves and roots on each of the plants. Spring is the best time to divide grasses, just as the new shoots are beginning to develop.

Many grasses can also be raised from seed, and many self-sown seedlings are often found growing around parent plants. Fresh seed can be sown in autumn or spring.

LAWNS

'A lawn complements whatever structures and plants you have in your garden.'

A
S A NATION, WE ARE sometimes accused of being obsessed with our lawns; an immaculate lush green swathe surrounded by colourful flowerbeds has been the aim of the British gardener for centuries. Despite modern trends for alternative garden surfaces, the lawn remains incredibly popular, and rightly so; few other ground coverings have so much going for them. A backdrop of verdant grass provides the perfect foil for surrounding plants, which look their best set against a velvety green canvas. Lawns are wonderfully cool and soft underfoot – and therefore exceptionally child-friendly – but can be remarkably durable with normal garden usage. Dig up the lawn and you will miss out on one of the most evocative of all gardening pleasures – the smell of freshly-cut grass.

On the other hand, lawns can soon look scrappy if not properly maintained, and their upkeep can be fairly labour intensive. The Royal Horticultural Society gardeners pride themselves on the quality of the lawns in their care; and, given the vast expanses of grass at each of the gardens and the hordes of visitors tramping over them throughout the year, it's hardly surprising they have developed their technique for keeping the turf in peak condition to a fine art. By selecting an appropriate type and quality of turf for the localized growing conditions and expected wear and tear, and following a regular maintenance programme, they succeed in producing enviably beautiful lawns, the rewards of which far outweigh the effort.

LEFT: The beautiful lawns in Lady Anne's Garden at RHS Garden Rosemoor add serenity to the surrounding *Thuja plicata* 'Irish Gold', *Robinia pseudoacaia frisia* and *Acer palmatum*. ABOVE: Fine lawn grass.

Lawns are as popular now as they were back in the 1300s when the idea of well-manicured expanses of grass became all the rage. Flowers might have more instant appeal with their bright and often gaudy colours, but a lawn can transport you to an altogether calmer plane, its cool green and even closely-clipped surface soothing and inviting you to stroll and relax. Creating and maintaining velvety turf requires time and attention, but it will prove to be time well spent.

A traditional family garden comprises a well-manicured lawn surrounded by shrubs and bedding plants.

Lawns from seed

Grass seed for all kinds of lawn is readily available from all garden retailers and is easy to sow – simply scatter the seeds at the recommended rate on the soil surface, and within a few days a hazy green patina will begin to appear. For a top-quality lawn, however, it pays to devote some care to the initial soil preparation well before sowing.

In early spring, when the soil is workable, dig over the site and remove all stones, builder's rubble and weed roots. Take out any severed tree roots too, as these may rot and cause potentially lethal fungal problems.

A month or two later, break down large soil clods by walking over the surface or pulverizing them with the back of a garden fork. If you choose a day for this when the surface is dry, you will not compact the soil and destroy its structure or impede drainage.

Make sure the surface is level, because bumps and hollows create problems when mowing. If you have deep topsoil, lower any raised areas and transfer the spare soil to hollows, but if the topsoil is shallow, import good quality soil or loam from turf suppliers and spread this to create a level surface.

Allow the soil to settle, preferably all summer, only removing any stones that appear on the surface. During this time weed seeds will germinate and overlooked roots regrow, but they are easy to pull out to leave a really clean site.

In early autumn rake the surface to a crumbly tilth with the texture of breadcrumbs. Make sure it is perfectly level by pulling a large plank across the surface; get someone to hold one end, then double check with a spirit level balanced on the plank edge. While still warm from summer but moist from autumn rain, the soil is now ready to accept seed.

Choose a calm, dry day when gentle rain is forecast sometime in the following week. Make a metre-square frame out of bamboo canes as a guide, and lay this on the surface.

Shake the box or bag of seed to mix the different types of grass seed. Weigh 50g (1oz) of seeds into a plastic cup, and mark the level to avoid further weighing. Scatter the seed evenly on the surface of the soil within the 1-metre square.

Sow in different directions to ensure the whole of the surface is sown with seed. When you have sown the whole area, cover the seed by gently raking the soil surface, again in two different directions to ensure good coverage. Seedlings will emerge within a fortnight.

Grass seed germinates quickly, often disturbing and lifting some of the surrounding soil. This should be gently rolled back into place when seedlings reach 5cm (2in) high, using a light roller such as that found at the rear of many cylinder mowers. Two days later you can make the first cut, removing the top 1.5cm (½in) using any mower with all its rollers removed. (Check when buying a mower that the rollers are easily removed. A basic tool kit and the user information will be needed. Some models have integral mowers that cannot be removed, whilst others have removable rollers to help maintenance of the machine.) The blades must be sharp to avoid tearing seedlings, roots and shoots, from the soil. Mow again a week later, at the same height, after which you can mow regularly with the mower at its usual setting. Do not walk

Heavy rolling is unnecessary for lawns and often compacts the soil,

leading to drainage problems. The light rollers at the back of many cylinder

mowers are preferable as they only push the grass leaves down gently.

unnecessarily on newly sown lawns until they are established. This can take up to year. Mowing and maintenance are essential but all other activities should be kept to a minimum.

You can buy special mixtures of lawn seed for shady areas. To help these grasses establish, mow the area less frequently and leave the blades on the mower higher than normal initially.

Choosing a mower

There is a mower to suit every purpose, from the traditional hand-pushed machine for small patches to ride-on mini-tractors for managing lawns by the hectare. Budget often determines the type of mower purchased, but it is equally important to match the machine to your lawn. A hand-pushed cylinder mower is ideal for a small lawn, provided it is kept sharp and well-oiled – the finish is often first-class and noise is minimal.

For larger lawns many gardeners choose electric mowers. Most are lightweight and effortless to use, but they require an outdoor power supply.

Electricity in the garden is potentially lethal, so you should protect yourself by making sure the mower is connected to a residual current device (RCD). Should you accidentally cut through the electricity cable, the RCD will turn off the power before it can cause injury. You can buy plug-in RCDs from garden retailers to protect the particular socket you are using, or employ a qualified electrician to wire one centrally into the house to cover all sockets.

Petrol-driven mowers are the choice for large lawns where it is impractical to run electricity. They are heavier than other pedestrian mowers, so

check you can easily manoeuvre one round your lawn – ask the retailer for a demonstration before buying. Generally more powerful and robust than electric mowers and free from the need to trail a cable round the lawn, they require regular maintenance and servicing to keep them working efficiently. These mowers usually come with different cutting widths, so check your mower is the right one for you before buying.

Ride-on mowers have wider cutting widths and are the best machines for extensive lawns, cutting large areas quickly and effectively, although they are heavy and can cause compaction on heavy soils. There are two main types: models with built-in seats are comfortable and easy, even fun, to drive, whereas mowers with separate trailing seats pulled by the mowing section are sometimes less comfortable and awkward to manoeuvre.

There is also a choice of cutting mechanism for all mowers:

Cylinder types cut with a similar action to scissors, with a varying number of blades mounted on a cylinder and cutting against a fixed edge – the more blades, the finer the cut. They produce the best finish but may be difficult to use when the grass is long or damp. Most cylinder mowers have grass collection boxes.

Rotary mowers have a horizontal metal or plastic blade spinning at high speed and cutting with a similar action to a scythe. The finish is good, even if the grass is long or damp, but not as fine as cylinder machines, and basic models do not have grass collection boxes. Rotary mowers that float across the ground on a cushion of air are perfect for uneven lawns, steep banks and for getting into tight corners.

The well-maintained lawns at RHS Garden Rosemoor enrich the surrounding borders as well as the landscape further afield.

A guide to mowing

Regular mowing is the only way to create a perfect lawn. In spring, autumn and early winter, cutting every week will keep the grass under control, while in summer, when growth is strong, twice-weekly mowings might be necessary to maintain a trim finish. Although frequent cutting may sound like a lot of work, it is better for the lawn and you will find it is easier to cut shorter grass more often than to struggle infrequently with long grass.

You should choose the finished height carefully. No lawn should be scalped closely, because the finer grasses find it hard to maintain adequate growth, allowing patches of bare soil to develop and host weed seeds and moss. At the other extreme a lawn that is allowed to grow over about 5cm (2in) tall is difficult to mow and will often look yellow after cutting, with some grass species never being encouraged to branch densely.

It is best to collect all lawn clippings during or after cutting, either in the grass collection box or by raking the surface after you have finished mowing. If left on the lawn in any quantity, they can become compacted and cause drainage problems. But never add thick layers of grass clippings to a compost heap, as they will settle in a black slimy mass. Mix them instead with a fibrous carbon-rich material such as torn paper, straw or coarse plant waste.

Sometimes it is impossible to mow regularly, and then you need to take special steps to maintain a fine finish.

Holidays

After a break of two weeks or more, the lawn will be overgrown. Do not give in to temptation and scythe down all the extra growth, because this will shock the grass plants and remove most of their food-producing leaves in one go. Instead, set the mower blades at their highest level and lightly trim the lawn. Two days later, set the blades slightly lower and cut again; then wait a further two days before mowing at the normal height.

Lawns from turf

Chris Rose is Supervisor of Turf and Machinery at RHS Garden Hyde Hall where he has full responsibility for the upkeep of their magnificent lawns.

A well-tended lawn can be a pivotal feature in a garden. As well as being an important space for recreation and relaxation, it creates an area of green tranquillity amid colourful flowers and jostling shrubs, a constant foil to the changing seasons and a soothing contrast to paths, walls and other hard aspects of the landscape. There are many kinds of lawn, from tough play area at one extreme to exquisite masterpiece of velvet turf at the other, but all start life in the same way, with careful site preparation to give the grass a good, long-lasting foundation for healthy growth.

Laying turves

1 After cultivating the site and leaving it to settle, prepare the surface for turfing by pricking it over with a garden fork, removing all roots and stones as you go. Tread firm and then rake in several directions until the surface is even – fill any hollows by raking or adding a layer of loam over the surface.

2 Lay the first turf at the edge of the lawn area, place a stout piece of board on top and tamp down firmly with the handle of a lumphammer. Lay the next turf so that it overlaps the first by about 5cm (2in). Cut through both turves with a serrated knife to obtain a tight joint. Continue until the first row is complete.

3 Lay the next row in the same way, staggering the joints like brickwork so that the lawn knits together quickly. When you have finished, brush sieved topsoil or old potting compost over all the joints to fill any gaps. Water the lawn every evening in dry weather until the turves are well rooted.

Chris's turf-buying guide

On delivery, check the turf closely. It should be moist, free from weeds and a healthy green – any signs of yellowing may indicate the turf has been rolled and stored for three or more days. Buying turf with long blades of grass can reveal hidden weeds, which can be removed before laying.

A one-metre length of turf should not break when held at arm's length by a short edge; if it does, reject the whole batch. All turf should be of equal thickness, which is important for a smooth even lawn.

Have the site ready before delivery, as rolled turf will only keep in good condition for two days. If you cannot lay it straight away, cover the turf with a sheet of plastic to retain water and provide shade. If the delay is longer than 2–3 days, unroll the turf on a firm surface in a cool, partially shaded position and water it every night.

Chris Rose has a key role at Hyde Hall, for nothing makes so instant an impact as a broad vista of well-maintained turf. Visitors often judge a garden by the quality of its lawns, so Chris has to keep his looking pristine every week of the year to make sure that vital first impression is one of approval and admiration. He strongly believes that 'a lawn complements whatever structures and plants you have in your garden.'

Tips from Hyde Hall

- Start by preparing the soil thoroughly as this is the only chance to get everything right.
- Buy top quality turf from a reputable dealer. Transforming poor turf into good can take a lot of coaxing, and may even prove impossible.
- Check turf on delivery and reject anything you are unhappy with.
- Watch the weather – ideally you want a dry day for laying, as it can be an unpleasant job in the wet, but you need rain soon after finishing.
- Take time over the work. Start with an even surface because reducing bumps and raising hollows after the turf is laid will be tricky.
- Stand on scaffolding boards or old floorboards while you work as they spread your weight across a larger area, avoiding deep footprints. Do not walk on freshly-laid turf for at least six weeks.

RHS KNOW-HOW

- Lift a turf at the edge of a newly-laid lawn to check for tiny white roots. This shows that the grass is rooting and establishing.
- Wait until the lawn has rooted before trimming it to shape. This avoids thin slivers of turf around the edges trying to root in possibly dry conditions.
- Fill any large gaps between turves with a mixture of sieved soil and grass seed.
- Do not use chemicals on a lawn until it has established for a year, then apply fertilizers, ideally in the autumn. Avoid using weedkillers for at least 18 months.
- Cover small lawns with horticultural fleece for a month after laying to protect the grass from fierce sun and light frosts.

If your grass develops brown tips, your mower could be to blame.
Blunt blades chew and bruise leaves, which then die back. Check blades
are sharp before every use and always clean them after cutting.

Wet grass

Avoid mowing when the lawn is wet. This can tear the grass blades, leaving an uneven finish, and may even be dangerous if you use an electric mower. You might also cause problems with drainage by trampling on the wet surface and compacting the soil. If you are unable to mow for any length of time, simply trim around the sides of the lawn with edging shears. This will leave a tidy respectable finish until you are able to mow again.

Drought

It would take an exceptionally long dry period to kill a lawn. A normal summer drought will turn most lawns yellow or brown, but they do recover, and watering established grass is not essential. Avoid mowing before a period of hot dry weather is forecast – longer grass covers the soil surface more effectively, reducing water evaporation, and survives a drought with less discoloration than closely cropped turf. Young grass seedlings and freshly laid turf do need water in a drought however, either from a fine rose on the end of a watering can or a lawn sprinkler set to fine mist.

Neglect

There are two choices when you are faced with an inherited lawn of poor quality. You can try to restore it with a regime of careful mowing, feeding, spot weeding and local re-seeding, but this may take time and will be only partially successful if the finer lawn grasses have been replaced with coarse species. Alternatively, you can dig up or rotavate the area and start again with seed or turf, usually the most economical option if the lawn comprises more than 50 per cent weeds.

Choosing grass seed

Select the best mixture from the wide range available according to the desired finish and intended use.

A hard-working lawn needs to be able to withstand heavy traffic, games and furniture, and seed mixtures for 'family', 'utility' or 'hardwearing' lawns are ideal for this. A major ingredient will be ryegrass, a robust species with wider leaf blades than other kinds, and an ability to survive frequent heavy wear. Most ryegrasses look less delicate than fine leaved species, but modern dwarf perennial ryegrasses still have a satisfying appearance, good colour and remarkable durability.

For a refined lawn with a bowling-green or snooker table finish, you will need to sow a mix of grass seed without any form of ryegrass. Fine species such as Chewings Fescue and Browntop produce a dense sward that is superb to look at but not as hardwearing as ryegrasses. With regular cutting – perhaps daily when growth is most active in spring and autumn – you can achieve a very high quality lawn.

Essential lawn calendar

Producing a great-looking lawn is a year-round project. Repeat maintenance is the key to success.

Spring

Although there may be a hint of spring as early as the end of February, you should resist any temptation to mow: severe weather often arrives late in the month, and freshly cut lawns are particularly susceptible to frost damage.

Start preparing the soil if you are planning a new lawn. You can sow seeds and lay turf throughout spring, but you might have to water frequently if the summer is dry. Alternatively, begin work on the site now, ready for making the lawn in the autumn.

Before you start mowing, brush all debris off the lawn and give it a gentle rake to raise all the grass blades ready for cutting. If you are aware of moss in your lawn, now is a good time to tackle it before the spring rain urges it on (see p156 for information on avoiding and tackling moss). The first cut of the year should be made with the blades of the mower set high so that it just removes the tips of the grass – anything more severe will reduce the strength of the grass and cause yellowing.

Feeding with a lawn fertilizer high in nitrogen can start late in April. Nitrogen encourages leaf growth and effects can be seen within a week, but remember that feeding will mean more mowing.

Summer

Mow the lawn more often, once or twice a week if growth demands it, but if the weather is dry, leave the grass long to preserve vigour and colour.

Weeds will be growing quickly now. You can spot-treat broad-leaved weeds with a lawn herbicide or remove them with a trowel, making sure you extract all the roots to prevent re-growth.

Even if your mower has a grass box, use a spring tine rake on fine lawns regularly to remove or disperse all grass clippings.

Continue feeding with nitrogen-rich fertilizer up to midsummer, after which you should stop encouraging further leaf growth.

Even in winter, the lawn looking down Battleston Hill at RHS Garden Wisley draws visitors to the mixed borders.

Autumn

This is the best time to sow lawn seed and lay turf, while the soil is warm and moist, with less chance of drought. Autumn is also a good time to prepare your lawn for spring by scarifying. Scarification is the energetic process of raking a lawn with a spring tine rake to remove condensed grass clippings and surface debris, called thatch. It requires downward pressure on the rake, and your lawn can look sorry for itself afterwards, but it will soon recover and produce many sideshoots. Scarifying in spring means that the grass will cover the gaps more quickly, but it can suffer some damage, or the gaps can be overrun by weeds before the grass gets going, so scarifying in autumn is often better.

Feed the lawn with a fertilizer high in potash to encourage strong root growth. Avoid nitrogenous feeds now because these encourage fresh sappy foliage that is easily damaged by frost.

Gradually reduce the frequency of mowing. A weekly cut should be enough.

Worm activity can increase and leave numerous casts on the surface. These are not harmful but may spoil a lawn's appearance – simply brush them across the surface, where they act as a top dressing of finely-sieved soil. Do not kill worms.

Relieve soil compaction by spiking with a garden fork. Push the tines 15cm (6in) into the soil and then brush loam-based seed compost into the holes. The compost will improve the soil structure and strengthen roots.

Winter

In warm dry weather an occasional trim with the mower can be beneficial if the grass is still growing. Book a service for a mower before the new season. Tidy up the sides with edging shears to leave the lawn neatly trimmed.

Brush or rake all leaves off the surface of the lawn – grass can die under a layer of fallen leaves.

You can still turf new lawns in early winter, if the weather is mild and wet, but never lay turf on frozen soil or when freezing weather is forecast.

Walking on frozen grass will kill turf and will leave black footprints as temperatures start to rise.

Chamomile lawns may develop brown patches after a wet winter,

especially if plants are beginning to age. Either replace affected

plants or confine the lawn to better-drained or sheltered areas.

Lawn alternatives

Grass is not the only material you can use to create a lawn. Many other plants will mat together, especially prostrate herbs. Although not as durable as turf, they can withstand light traffic and surround you with fragrance as you tread across their foliage. The two most popular choices are thyme and chamomile, both of them capable of providing colour and interest all year.

Chamomile

Chamaemelum nobile, the Roman or garden chamomile, and its non-flowering sport 'Treneague' (lawn chamomile) are the two varieties to plant, separately or in combination, if you want a relatively easy chamomile lawn. Both need acidic soil that is never waterlogged.

Sow seeds of *C. nobile* in March, and transplant the seedlings 15cm (6in) apart in early summer. Set out plants of 'Treneague' in well-prepared soil in spring or early summer. Keep them watered in dry weather and they will quickly knit together. *C. nobile* produces beautiful white and yellow daisy-like flowers in summer, particularly attractive in the double form 'Flore Pleno'. The only maintenance required is a two-monthly high cut.

Thyme

A very popular choice for its low maintenance needs and dense growth, thyme grows freely in most well-drained soils and tolerates hot dry conditions. Creeping thymes flower in summer, and the only pruning required is a single cut with a line trimmer or shears to remove their fading blooms and encourage branching. Do not expect a perfectly

level surface because plants will grow at different rates, even if they are all the same variety, but you will produce an exciting patchwork of white, pink or red flowers over aromatic evergreen leaves.

Raise the plants from cuttings and transplant them in spring. You might need to replace some of them every few years, so have a supply of new young plants ready as reinforcements. Varieties include the British native *Thymus polytrichus* subsp. *britannicus* for beautiful pink flowers or its white form 'Thomas's White', or *Thymus serpyllum*.

A mixed thyme lawn adds both colour and scent to a garden scheme.

Bulbs for lawns

David Eggelton is the Senior Supervisor of the Ornamental Department whose job is to organize and maintain the ornamental gardens at the RHS Garden at Harlow Carr.

If you prefer a more natural-looking lawn, but don't want to go the whole hog and create a wildflower meadow, planting bulbs in the turf is a neat, but attractive compromise and can brighten up an otherwise dull lawn. Naturalizing bulbs is not as technical a procedure as it sounds, it is simply a way of growing bulbs so that they look as though they belong and just happened to be there.

David Eggelton believes that creating a 'natural' corner in any garden is extremely rewarding – both for the gardener and for the local wildlife. Although the garden at Harlow Carr is fortunate in that it has vast areas of grass that can easily be devoted to bulbs; it doesn't necessarily follow that you need a lot of space to naturalize bulbs – even a small area of a lawn will do.

Naturalizing bulbs in the lawn

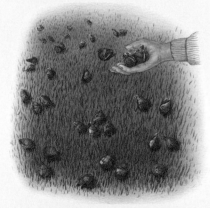

1 Select the area where you want to naturalize bulbs, gather a few in your hands and throw them into the air, letting them fall naturally to the ground. Then, using a bulb planter, remove a plug of soil for the bulbs.

2 Plant the bulbs, pointed end up, in these holes at a depth of three times the height of the individual bulbs, depending on their size and type. Replace the plug of soil and press it down with your foot to ensure contact with the bulb.

3 If you are planting a lot of bulbs, slice through the turf and fold it back to reveal the soil. Plant bulbs in the soil, fold back the turf and stamp down to ensure a neat finish and contact with the bulbs.

Dividing in the green

Bluebells, anemones and snowdrops are best planted 'in the green'. This process involves planting something that is already in growth as opposed to dry, dormant bulbs. You can buy plants 'in the green' from specialist nurseries, or you can divide existing clumps.

1 Once flowering has finished, carefully lift an established clump of snowdrops using a hand fork. Gently tease apart offshoots from the main stem.

2 The new clumps will consist of upto five bulbs with their leaves. Replant elsewhere in the lawn at the same depth as the original planting. This is visible as a blanched area on the stems. Firm the soil and water.

Narcissi for every situation

Narcissus is a favourite for naturalizing – swathes of yellow trumpets lift the spirits in spring. To ensure success, consider carefully which variety is best for your situation: dainty, low growing varieties will be swamped by tall grass, and taller plants will look bullish in short grass.

In taller grass, varieties with large trumpets are best. *Narcissus* 'Carlton' is a sturdy yellow bloom and 'Actaea' is showy with white petals and lemon trumpets ringed with orange-red.

In short grass, go for varieties with small stems and trumpets. Try 'Jack Snipe', with narrow, milk-white petals and yellow trumpets; 'Minnow', with fragrant lemon-yellow trumpets and creamy yellow petals; or the wild daffodil or Lent lily, *Narcissus pseudonarcissus*, with its nodding straw-yellow petals and deeper yellow trumpets.

RHS KNOW-HOW

- Aim to produce drifts of single bulb varieties, not a dolly mixture of colours and species.
- Water bulbs when the autumn is dry and the soil is like dust. This enables the bulbs to establish quickly.
- Avoid weed- and mosskillers, aerate the soil and spike in bulb-planted areas.
- Avoid fertilizers – naturalized bulbs are happy without any artificial stimulants.
- Allow bulb leaves to yellow and start to decompose before mowing the grass.

EDIBLES

'There's nothing better in gardening than eating the fruits of your labour.'

Growing your own fruit and vegetables brings a sense of satisfaction that is hard to match in other areas of gardening. As we become increasingly concerned about where the produce on our plate originates, being able to track it from seed to table is a real bonus. Freshly picked home-grown strawberries bear little relation to the blandness of those air-freighted in, and popping newly harvested peas from their pods is an entirely different experience to opening a bag from the freezer cabinet. Even the smallest garden can incorporate edibles, with many varieties suitable for containers, or dotting among ornamental plants. Nothing beats growing your own for sheer freshness, choice and flavour, and for children; the thrill of eating something they have nurtured from seedlings is incalculable.

All the Royal Horticultural Society Gardens have areas dedicated to growing edible plants. Their orchards billow with blossom in spring and burgeon with fruit by late summer. Top fruits are also impeccably trained into fans, espaliers and stepovers, soft fruits glisten through the protective netting of fruit cages, and row upon row of vegetables bring decorative qualities to the productive garden. The crops glow with health and vitality and are as beautiful to look at as any flower garden. For the average gardener whose aim is to create an attractive fruit and vegetable patch, and provide fresh food for the table, there could be no better source of inspiration and information than the gardeners who tend these crops so lovingly.

LEFT: The productive and attractive vegetable garden at RHS Garden Rosemoor in August.
ABOVE: Autumn fruiting Raspberry 'Zeva'.

Growing for the kitchen can become compulsive once you have experienced the excellence of produce raised under your own control. You can choose the varieties, plan how much of each crop to grow and when, decide whether to cultivate them organically or by using more chemical methods, and finally harvest the results in peak condition. You even have the option of growing them in a special area of the garden or blending them into existing flower beds and shrub borders: many have ornamental foliage, flowers or fruits, and can be decorative as well as productive features. All you need to do is satisfy a few basic requirements.

Organized, well-grown and ultimately tasty – the vegetables in narrow beds at RHS Garden Rosemoor.

LEFT: Sun-ripened on the tree – the best way to eat Victoria plums.

The essentials

Perhaps more than most other plant types, food crops need the right conditions for success – match the soil, light levels and aspect to the needs of what you want to grow, and you are halfway to success.

Food plants are grown to be cropped, and you will be removing large portions, whether foliage, fruit or some other part, for consumption and then clearing away the rest of the plant after harvest. To get the best quality crops in reasonable quantities and, in the case of many vegetables, fairly quick yields, you need to supply enough extra fertility in the soil to sustain all the energy the plant is going to invest in growth. Much of the answer lies in the soil. Good balanced fertility feeds strong plants and a well structured soil ensures fast unchecked growth. Plants growing healthily are less prone to attack by pests and diseases. Add a warm sunny position and adequate moisture, and you will have satisfied their basic needs.

Organic matter is the secret of growing healthy crops of all kinds, even though it rarely contains high levels of nutrients. Adding rotted horse or farmyard manure, spent mushroom compost or home-made garden compost to the soil improves its structure, enabling beneficial bacteria, fungi, worms and other invertebrates to thrive, multiply and naturally improve the environment for your crops. Better structure means, among other things, less waterlogging in heavy soils and greater water retention in sandy soils.

Whether you dig these organic supplements into the soil in winter or spread them as a mulch in spring, worms and other soil organisms and weather between them will break them down into valuable humus and nutrients that gradually become incorporated throughout the soil. Additional fertilizers such as bonemeal, seaweed extract or, if you prefer, concentrated chemical feeds are only needed to boost the growth of hungry crops. Never add animal manure and spent mushroom compost to the soil at the same time. Although excellent sources of organic matter on their own, in combination they can cause a chemical reaction due to the presence of lime in the mushroom compost which releases gasses that harm plant roots. Applying manure and garden lime together has the same effect.

Most edible crops need an open, fairly sunny site to thrive. If positioned close to large overhanging trees, vegetables will not do well as they will be deprived of light, water and nutrients, while herbs will be deficient in their distinctive aromatic oils. Check the garden over the course of a year and note how light levels change as leaf canopies expand. Remember that some crops grow quite tall, and sweetcorn or runner beans, for example, can cast shade over other vegetables, so you should plan carefully to avoid causing problems, although plants such as lettuces may welcome this extra shade in midsummer. Grow fast-cropping plants, such as radish, near slower or taller vegetables.

Rotating crops between small beds ensures healthy plants.

wooden boards to help retain the soil within the cropping area, especially when the surface level begins to rise with the annual dressings of organic matter which, over a period of a few years, will dramatically increase fertility.

These beds can fit neatly between trained fruit trees (cordons, fans, etc) or rows of soft fruit, and can be edged with small trailing plants such as prostrate or short herbs like marjoram, chives and the various kinds of thyme. Leave sufficient space between beds for paths that allow comfortable access – these may be wide enough for a wheelbarrow or just a narrow strip for you to walk along, and can be constructed from many different materials. On allotments grass is often used, but this needs mowing and edging regularly, and in ornamental gardens gravel, grit, slate or paving slabs may be preferable laid over geotextile or landscape fabric to suppress weeds.

Vegetable beds

The way crops are laid out has changed since the era of large kitchen gardens, and long rows of vegetables are going out of fashion. The soil in between is regularly trodden and compacted in the course of routine cultivation, and as a result requires digging every autumn. Growing vegetables in beds, however, often results in higher yields with lower maintenance – plants are closely spaced, thus smothering weeds, shading the soil and reducing moisture loss, and the soil isn't walked over.

Vegetable beds should be narrow enough so you can reach the centre easily from either side without treading on them. In practice this means about 1.2m (4ft) wide, depending on your reach. The sides of the beds are easily constructed from

Choosing crops

Deciding what to grow is important when planning a productive garden. Allotments often supply enough space for you to grow a little of everything, although even there it will be difficult to achieve self-sufficiency. On smaller plots or areas incorporated within a garden, you need to be very selective and, for maximum yields, choose dwarf, fast-growing or smaller leaved crops that can be grown closer together. That way you should get more variety from restricted space.

Some crops, especially herbs and many trained fruits, are particularly decorative and may be incorporated into flower beds as highlights or edging. The soft ferny foliage of carrots and parsley, for example, is equally as attractive as

Traditional 'heritage' varieties, can be tastier than many new introductions.
By growing some of the older kinds, valuable genetic qualities are kept in
circulation, such as disease-resistance or simply greater flavour.

cosmos leaves, with the bonus of a nutritious edible crop, while Swiss chard has dramatic leaves and vividly coloured stems that look stunning in any ornamental border, especially if combined with the rich purple of beetroot foliage.

There is little point in devoting ground to crops that are more easily grown on a field scale, such as swedes and maincrop potatoes, or those that are relatively cheap to buy in supermarkets and farmshops. It makes sense to concentrate instead on your favourite foods, especially those generally unobtainable elsewhere or that have superior quality when harvested really fresh. Sugar levels in sweetcorn, for example, start to decline very quickly and cobs eaten within hours of picking have supreme flavour.

An important part of your plan is an honest assessment of how much time you can devote to gardening. Some crops need more attention than others: to get a good head of celery takes care, high fertility and lavish watering, and cauliflowers are almost as demanding. Beans, radishes, carrots and potatoes on the other hand are all relatively low-maintenance crops, while shallots and onions grown from sets are among the easiest vegetable to grow – you simply plant immature bulbs in spring and harvest them when mature in summer or early autumn.

Crop rotation

By ensuring that a particular vegetable is not grown in the same place year after year, traditional crop rotation prevents a harmful build-up of pests and diseases, and the depletion of nutrients that crop might need.

Rotation is easy to carry out and involves dividing the vegetable plot into three sections. In the first year, root crops are grown in one section and cabbages and other brassicas in another, with beans, peas and everything else grown in the final section. The following year the root crops are moved to where the brassicas grew, brassicas are transferred to the beans and 'everything else' section and all other crops move to the former roots section. In the third year, the groups move on one more section, so providing a three-year break before they return to the start of the sequence.

On smaller plots where division into sections is impractical, some kind of crop rotation plan is still advisable. You could grow root crops one year, followed by leafy crops the next, or simply make sure that you do not grow the same crop in the same place in two consecutive seasons. If you can follow this pattern, pests and diseases will never have more than a single growing season in which to become established, while nutrients are depleted and added at manageable rates.

Root vegetables

Sandy, stone-free soil is the ideal for carrots, parsnips and long beetroots, all of which prefer unrestricted growth in deep soil where their roots can search freely for water. Do not despair if you have shallow, heavy or stony soil, though, because stump-rooted varieties are available with smaller, shorter roots that develop satisfactorily in as little as 10cm (4in) of stone-free topsoil.

Root vegetables are excellent for mopping up residual nutrients left in the soil after other crops have been harvested, and produce better quality roots in this way. Unlike most other vegetables, which revel in well-manured conditions, root crops do not like too much nitrogen and respond to lavish manuring by producing forked or distorted roots – although still edible, these are difficult to dig up intact and even harder to prepare for the pot.

Potatoes

Potatoes are more adaptable, robust plants and will usually produce superb crops in most soil types, especially if you can dig in some home-made compost prior to planting. They are root vegetables, but can be planted separately as they are the ideal pioneer crop for breaking up fresh ground before growing other vegetables. This is due to the fact that digging their planting trenches opens up uncultivated soil, while any added compost and manure will improve the structure of the soil.

During cultivation, the stems of potatoes are gradually covered with soil ('earthing up'), which further loosens the surface, reducing weeds by bringing weed seeds to the surface so the seedlings can be removed, and exposing pests to natural predators. The ground is cultivated once more as you fork up the harvest of tubers, when weeds are finally cleared and the soil broken up, ready for sowing or planting other vegetables at the start of the next season.

Increased fertility of the soil in the raised timber beds helps leek 'Newton F1' produce fantastic results at RHS Garden Rosemoor.

Legumes

This group, including peas and beans, are easy and valuable crops because their root systems can take nitrogen out of the atmosphere and store it in the soil, where it will often remain as a fertilizer for your next crop. You can grow them as an additional group in a rotation scheme, fitting them before brassicas to provide them with extra food when their turn comes round, or they can be integrated into flower beds. Their blooms are so attractive, they combine well with annuals and perennials in a cottage-style garden.

There is a large selection of types and varieties that will ensure a long cropping season. They grow well in most soil types, but prefer plenty of organic matter forked deeply into the ground to help keep their roots moist. Never let plants dry out in summer, and always pick the pods regularly before they mature – they will taste much sweeter and plants go on to form more flowers and pods, whereas leaving pea or bean pods to mature will make the plant switch off flower production.

Brassicas

Cauliflowers, cabbages, Brussels sprouts, turnips, Swedes, kale and kohl rabi are all members of the brassica family, which can be a challenge to grow successfully in some soils. They must grow continuously from seedling stage to harvest, because any check to growth – a cold spell, for example, or period of drying out – will cause plants to run to seed ('bolt') prematurely. Never let plants dry out for more than a day or two. You can avoid this by adding plenty of organic matter during soil preparation and mulching after planting but only when the soil is moist.

The crinkly leaves of kale 'Nero di Toscana' combine well with runner bean 'Hammond's Dwarf Scarlet' at RHS Garden Rosemoor, proving vegetables can look as good as they taste.

Most brassicas prefer consolidated soil, particularly cabbages and Brussels sprouts which are expected to produce firm hearts. Leave the ground to settle for several weeks after digging – if possible, cultivate in the autumn and plant in spring. Compact the soil by walking over it before planting, and then firm in the transplants with your feet or fists. A good test for firm planting is to tug one of the leaves: if it tears, all is well, but if you can pull the plant out of the soil, it is too loose.

Brassicas take a lot of nutrients out of the soil, but if they follow beans or peas they can benefit from the residual nitrogen. Manure or compost the site generously, and give over-wintered crops a supplementary feed in late spring with a balanced organic fertilizer, such as seaweed extract. They also need lime and won't grow well in acid soils. Test the site with a soil testing kit if you are not sure of its condition, and adjust its pH status.

Garden herbs

Some of the most versatile of all plants, herbs will flourish happily in existing beds and borders as ornamentals, or you can group them together in part of the vegetable area or in a separate herb garden. They also do well in containers indoors or outside.

Matching soil conditions to the type of herb is the key to success. Many have their origins in Mediterranean regions, where the air is warm and dry, the soil well-drained, even poor, and the light is bright. For best results you need to grow these herbs – which include sage, thyme, marjoram, lavender and most silver or grey-leaved species – well away from any shade or wet clay. Other herbs such as lovage, parsley, angelica, bergamot and comfrey grow better in heavy soil than in light sandy soil. Between these two extremes lie the majority of garden soils, various kinds of loam that combine sand and clay in different ratios. Basil, chives, coriander and dill all enjoy these conditions.

It does not matter if your soil is less than perfect. You can improve the drainage of clay to provide the optimum conditions for fennel, by adding plenty of grit to leaven the heaviness. Similarly organic matter such as leafmould or garden

compost can be blended into light soil if you want to grow superb mint. Most herbs are surprisingly resilient and will grow well, if not lavishly, in average conditions. Alternatively you can keep them in pots of appropriately matched compost, a safer option for potentially invasive herbs such as mint and tarragon. As a decorative bonus, herbs in containers can be moved round the garden as and when the plants are looking their best or are required for fresh harvest next to a barbecue.

Easy herbs

Herbs are some of the easiest edibles crops to grow and maintain, and these are a few favourites:

Basil (*Ocimum* vars.) is available in a multitude of flavours such as lemon, lime and cinnamon, as well as the plain sweet green kind. All are easy to grow from seed, provided you remember they need a well-drained soil and a warm, sunny position. Frost is lethal, but you can maximize crops by sowing early under glass for planting out in late spring, while late plants can be moved to a cool greenhouse in autumn.

Borage (*Borago officinalis*) produces beautiful blue flowers in summer and young leaves with a mild cucumber flavour. It dislikes being moved, so sow the seeds where you want plants to flower, in a sunny spot on well-drained, sandy soil.

Coriander (*Coriandrum sativum*), an essential ingredient of curries and chutneys, has pungent leaves and warmly aromatic seeds. Sow in well-drained soil and a sunny position where you want the plants to grow, because transplanting can cause premature flowering.

Chervil (*Anthriscus cerefolium*) leaves taste like a blend of aniseed and parsley, and are used extensively in French cooking. A semi-shaded spot in well-drained soil packed with organic matter is best. Only use fresh seed as it loses its viability after a year.

Chives (*Allium schoenoprasum*) provide a mild onion flavour and are one of the easiest perennial herbs to grow in almost any soil and also in containers. To keep leaves succulent and tasty, grow plants in a sunny spot, never let them dry out and do not pick all their leaves in one go.

Dill (*Anethum graveolens*) is a popular accompaniment for fish dishes. Easy to grow from seed, it is best in a sheltered position with plenty of sun. Regular cutting will encourage fresh growth.

Lemongrass (*Cymbopogon citratus*) is a popular tender herb that looks dramatic as a pot plant for a cool greenhouse. The white, bulbous base to the leaves is used to flavour many dishes. Well-drained compost, plenty of sun and winter warmth are the prerequisites for success. These plants must never suffer frost though.

Marjoram (*Origanum vulgare*) is an easy indispensable herb that grows well in containers, and can seed itself lavishly in well-drained soil and sunny, sheltered positions. Leave it to flower, because it is a favourite bee plant.

Mint (*Mentha spicata*) is grown for decorative and culinary use. It grows best in a sunny or shady position and in a well-drained soil, but beware, it can be rampant when left unrestricted, and will riot through beds and borders, even penetrating lawns. Confine plants by burying a bottomless container so that only 2.5cm (1in) protrudes above soil level – the container needs to be at least 30cm (12in) deep to allow adequate downward root growth and sufficient soil to supply nutrients and drainage. Plant in the centre of the container, and the mint will root freely as far as the sides, which will act as a physical barrier. Should any shoots bridge this, simply pull them off – they can be potted up in containers of soil-less multipurpose compost for out of season use indoors or in the greenhouse.

Sorrel (*Rumex acetosa*) can be used sparingly to add flavour to soups and sauces. It grows best in acid soils with plenty of organic matter. If flower heads appear on young plants, remove them to preserve the flavour of the leaves and prevent self-seeding.

Thyme (*Thymus* species and vars.) is available in a number of guises, from creeping, caraway-flavoured and woolly, to white or golden variegated. All enjoy being grown in containers or outdoors in soil that is low in nutrients – use seed compost for potting, and only water when necessary to keep plants alive since this will concentrate flavour, as does a position in full sun.

Fruit in the garden

Fruit is something many gardeners are wary of introducing into the garden. Perhaps images of raspberries trained in long rows, apple trees tall enough to require a ladder at harvest time, and endless beds of pick-your-own strawberries all suggest that huge amounts of land are necessary to make the enterprise worthwhile. Traditional and commercial fruit growing does indeed demand a lot of room, but you do not need acres of ground to produce useful quantities of fruit from modern compact trees and bushes, and most kinds will even grow happily and yield well in containers. At RHS Wisley the skilled gardeners have proved that good cultivation and careful training can coax profusion from limited spaces.

Tree fruits

Apples and pears spring to mind when planning tree fruits and one or two trees in an average-sized garden will supply plenty of fresh fruit. Trees are a long term investment and there are plenty of considerations. Figs, plums and cherries are easily grown in Britain and, with protection, you can also get substantial crops from nectarines and apricots.

The eventual size of a tree depends on its rootstock, but whatever the size, there are basic requirements to successful growth. Fertile soil is essential, in which case very few additional fertilizers are required, but digging in plenty of organic matter will get your trees off to a flying start. Give fruit trees plenty of light and water, and avoid positions where the roots will compete for water and nutrients.

Choosing apples

The range of apple varieties is enormous and many gardeners worry about selecting the right ones for their garden. The first step is to visit an apple-tasting event in the autumn and sample as many fruits as you can to narrow down your options – there is no point devoting money, time and energy to growing an apple tree if you don't really like its fruit.

Size is another important consideration. Like some other tree fruits, apples can become large and unmanageable on their own roots, and so they are grafted onto a rootstock that determines the size, vigour and also the yield of the tree. These rootstocks range from extremely dwarfing, producing miniature trees and small crops of high quality fruit early in their lives, to vigorous for full-size orchard trees with potentially huge crops that take several years to reach maximum yields. Those you are likely to find are M27, which produces a tree about 2m (6ft) high; M9, 3m (10ft); M26, 4m (13ft) and MM106, 6m (20ft). Nurseries can also supply MM111 and M2, both 7m (23ft) or more. Always check the label when buying to make sure your tree will fit the available space.

As with all fruit, apple production depends on effective pollination at flowering time. Most apple varieties produce pollen that can only be used to fertilize the flowers of others, and even those few that are partially self-fertile, such as 'James Grieve', produce heavier crops if pollinated by another variety, so you need to plant at least two kinds unless there are already neighbouring trees growing nearby. A few, like 'Bramley's Seedling', do not produce much pollen, so they need two partners to ensure each tree will be fertilized.

Obviously they need to be in bloom together. Since apples flower over a long period, they are divided into groups – early, mid-season, mid-season/late and late-flowering – and varieties from any one group or two adjacent groups will usually be in flower at the same time. This variation in flowering time allows you to match varieties to your particular locality. Frost can seriously injure blooms, especially when fully open, and low temperatures discourage pollinating insects, but if you choose late-flowering varieties such as 'Laxton's Superb', 'Lord Derby' or 'Ellison's Orange', they are more likely to miss the frosts and set satisfactory crops.

Varieties also fruit at different times. Early kinds, which mature from late August onwards, generally need eating within a few weeks of picking, whereas late varieties, sometimes not fully ripe until November or later, can often be stored in a cool place for many months. It is a good idea when choosing varieties to balance your selection between these kinds to avoid a glut at any time and to spread the crop over as long a period as possible. You can also choose a mixture of eating and cooking apples for the fullest range of fruit.

The most common problem with many fruit trees is a fantastic, trug-busting crop one year followed by a miserly offering the next – this isn't due to any pests or diseases, but is something that is inherent in many varieties. One way to avoid this situation is to thin out fruit in early to mid summer to prevent excessive production; another way is to ensure that all your fruit trees are well-mulched and watered regularly during the early years of development.

Training fruit trees

Jonathan Keyte is a Senior Supervisor in the Fruit Department at RHS Garden Wisley. He has more than two decades of experience in the fruit industry, and during that time has trained and pruned hundreds of fruit trees.

Nothing tastes better than sun-ripened fruit freshly picked from your own plants. Their cultural requirements are very similar to those of any other food crop, except when it comes to training. A well-trained fruit tree is a work of art, is easier to maintain and ultimately produces better quality crops. The fruit trees at RHS Garden Wisley are superb examples of how to grow fruit in an orchard situation and also how to train them to grow well in small gardens.

Working with his team, Jonathan produces fruit for the public to try at apple-tasting days – important dates for your diary. Training fruit is considered by some gardeners to be difficult, but there are simple techniques – many handed down over generations – to help you achieve success, and Jonathan knows them all. He makes the business of growing fruit sound fun and much easier than you might think. 'There's nothing better in gardening than eating the fruits of your labour.'

Why train fruit?

There are three reasons for training fruit. In the first place, trained trees produce more top-quality fruit than those left to grow naturally. Horizontal branches flower and fruit more prolifically than those growing vertically, but much tree growth is upright, so gardeners need to know how and when to adjust these tendencies to their benefit. Training fruit is also a satisfying skill to practice, with almost certain results if you do it right. And lastly, trained fruit looks great in the garden.

Tree forms

Fruit trees can be trained in many different shapes.
- A bush is the most common form of fruit tree, with a bare 90cm (3ft) trunk branching at the top to form the framework of the tree. The final size will depend on the vigour of its rootstock.
- A cordon is usually a single-stemmed tree grown at an angle of 45° and tied to a cane or wires. This is an economical way to fit several trees, mostly apples or pears, into a small space. Upright and multi-stemmed cordons are also possible.
- An espalier has one or more pairs of horizontal branches arranged in tiers and trained to each side. A decorative way to produce superb apples and pears, it is easy to maintain because each branch is treated in the same way as a cordon.
- A fan-trained tree can be quite large but occupies little ground space because it grows flat on a wall or wire framework, with its branches rising from a short trunk and spreading out like a fan. Suitable for apples, pears, cherries, peaches or plums.

Pruning a bush tree

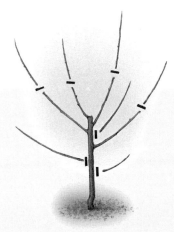

1 After one year's growth, in the winter, choose four strong branches that are well spaced on the tree – these are the primary branches. Prune these to half their length, cutting just above an outward-facing bud. Completely remove all other branches.

2 The next winter, prune all main branches by half the current season's growth. Remove any misplaced branches growing in the centre.

3 In the third winter, cut back leading branches by a half, together with lateral branches on the inside of the tree. A sturdy framework is now developing and will soon start producing fruit.

Technical terms

Fruit growing has its own set of mysterious expressions, which you should be familiar with to fully understand pruning and training.

- Apical bud. The largest bud growing at the tip of a branch, sometimes called a terminal bud.
- Bare-rooted. A tree without any soil around its roots. Usually bought in autumn and winter, it needs planting before spring.
- Basal cluster. A group of leaves near the base of a shoot, growing close together and sometimes crowded in a ring.
- Central leader. Often simply called the leader, this is the main shoot growing vertically.
- Lateral. A sideshoot or branch growing out from the central leader.
- Self-fertile. Describes a variety that does not require a pollinating partner to produce fruit.
- Spur. A slow-growing sideshoot, always short, that produces the flowers and fruit.
- Sublateral. A sideshoot growing from a lateral.

Jonathan's favourite apples

'Adam's Pearmain' is an old, late dessert variety with handsome red fruits and a dry, nutty flavour. Stores from November until February, but best around Christmas.

'Discovery', an early dessert variety with crisp red fruits that only store for a month from August and are best eaten straight from the tree.

'Edward VII' is a late culinary apple. The green, acidic, mild-flavoured fruits store from December until April.

'Ellison's Orange' is a mid-season aromatic apple with a taste of aniseed.

'Lord Lambourne', is a mid-season dessert with greenish, red-flushed fruits, and keeps from September to November.

'Saturn' is a sweet, self-fertile dessert apple has good resistance to scab and partly self-fertile. It can be stored from September until February.

'Sunset', a compact mid-season variety with good disease resistance, has aromatic, red-striped golden apples keeping from October until December.

'Winston' is a late dessert with yellow-green fruit. It is partly self-fertile and will store from October to December.

Pruning techniques

To train a bush plant, prune back the leader to 75cm (30in) above soil level after first planting it, cutting above a strong bud. Mulch around its base with well-rotted manure, leafmould or compost, ensuring the mulch does not touch the stem. Then follow the illustrated steps for pruning a bush tree that appear on the previous page.

A cordon tree requires slightly more complex training. The plant should be planted at an angle of 45° against wires tensioned between supports. Cut back any side shoots to three buds. The first summer (August/September) after planting, cut back lateral growths to three leaves above the basal cluster and any sublaterals to one leaf above the basal cluster. Continue pruning in this way every August/September.

Before planting a fan tree attach wires, 15cm (6in) apart, on a wall or between supports, and tension them with straining bolts. Then plant the 'maiden' (one-year-old) tree and cut back the leader to 45cm (18in) from soil level, just above a strong bud. During the first summer, train each of the two sideshoots against canes tied in at 45°. In August/September prune the sublaterals to three buds past the basal cluster. The following winter, cut back the two laterals by two-thirds to an upward-facing bud. In the second summer, select four strong shoots on each side branch. Tie these to canes fanned out on the wires. The lowest shoot will be almost horizontal. Do not allow any laterals to grow vertically in the centre of the fan at this stage. Late the following winter, cut each of the four leaders back by a third. During the third summer, select three strong shoots on each of the pruned leaders, fan these out and tie them to bamboo canes. Then, the next winter, cut all the leaders back by a quarter. Trim back any other shoots that are needed to provide vigorous growth and fill available space.

An espalier tree is trained on wires spaced 45cm (18in) apart on the wall or between supports, and secured with straining bolts and involves a slightly more complicated procedure.

Pruning an espalier

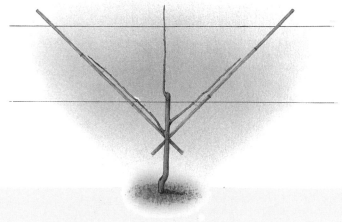

1 Attach three canes to the wires just below two sideshoots and the base of the leader; arrange two canes at 45° and the third vertically. Tie two sideshoots to the angled canes, one each side of the leader – which is tied to the vertical cane. The first summer, tie in the sideshoots and leader and cut any shoots growing from the trained branches to three buds above their basal cluster. Remove any other branches from the main shoot.

2 The next winter, untie the sloping branches and lower them to a horizontal wire; remove the canes and tie in the branches. Later the same winter, cut back the leader 45cm (18in) beyond the lower arms, trimming it above three strong buds. Cut back the horizontal shoots by a third, at a bud pointing downwards.

3 Early the next spring, repeat the procedure with a fresh set of canes to train the next two strong sideshoots and the upright leader. Continue this process until the tree has filled its allotted space. After that, trim back the leader and all horizontals to one bud past the basal cluster.

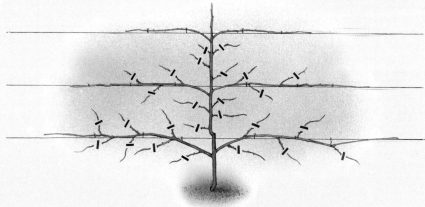

What to buy

Partly fan-trained trees can be expensive, so it can be preferable to buy a 'maiden' tree. Prune it after planting by cutting the leading shoot back to 45cm (18in) above the ground; if you cut just above a strong bud, the tree will quickly establish. If you choose an espalier, buy one that already has two tiers, saving you a lot of trial and error, and you could get fruit within two years of planting. Bush fruit trees are readily available as bare-root specimens in autumn and winter, or in containers throughout the year. At RHS Garden Wisley one-year-old bare-root trees regularly outperform older container-grown trees.

RHS KNOW-HOW

- When growing fruit against a wall or fence, position the trees 15cm (6in) away from the upright surface to allow good air circulation.
- Do not prune in freezing weather, which exposes trees to frost damage in open wounds and possible disease infection.
- Remove immature fruits from apple trees less than three years old. This helps them concentrate on growth and building up their vigour, and will result in better crops.

Pears for gardens

The range of pear varieties is smaller than that of apples, and if you garden in a cold or exposed area the choice diminishes further because pears flower a little earlier, when the risk of frost and cold winds is greater, and need more warmth and sunshine to produce well-flavoured fruits. There is not such an extensive range of rootstocks either, and only two are generally available: Quince A is the usual one, producing trees 3–6m (10–20ft) high according to variety and fertility, while Quince C is a little smaller, but needs richer soil.

Like apples, most pears need partners flowering at the same time – early, mid-season or late – to ensure pollination.

'Conference' is very reliable, flowering in mid-season and capable of producing heavy crops of long, juicy olive green fruits under most conditions. It is partially self-fertile but benefits from a compatible partner. The fruits should be harvested in late September and can be used until November.

'Concorde', a cracking late-season flowering variety with pale green fruits which melt in the mouth, has all the qualities of 'Conference' with enhanced flavour and heavy crops early in life. The fruits, harvested in late October, can be stored until December.

'Durondeau' is a compact variety and one of the best for smaller gardens. It flowers at mid-season, producing long fruits with juicy flesh in September which can be used until November, and as a bonus good autumn leaf colour.

'Winter Nelis' is a heavy cropper, with slender growth and late flowers that resist frost. Its long, green flavoursome fruits can be picked in late October and stored into January.

'Beth' produces golden russetted fruits that are small and variable in shape, but their flavour and melting texture is outstanding. The fruits can be picked in late August and used until September. It is an upright tree, flowering at mid-season.

'Jargonelle' is happy in colder areas. It flowers in mid-season and produces greenish-yellow fruits that are blushed with red and produced in good quantities, but it needs two pollen partners. The fruit is ready to be picked in early August and will keep for another month.

'Doyenné du Comice' is only for mild areas, away from cold winds. It does not produce a regular crop, but when it does the flavour, texture and class are supreme. It will flower late in the season and any fruits it produces will be ready for picking in October and can be stored until December.

*Figs are ripe when a drop of sticky juice oozes from the base of the fruit. Plums
are ready when they are easily picked from the tree, leaving their stalks behind,
but apples and pears can deteriorate quickly in store if their stalks are pulled off.*

Peaches and nectarines

Furry and smooth-skinned types respectively of
the same species, peaches and nectarines are self-
fertile summer fruits that will crop heavily in
warm sheltered situations with good drainage, but
they can prove difficult to cultivate outdoors in
colder areas. One of the most reliable ways to
grow them is to train a fairly early variety as a fan
against a sunny wall, where it will receive extra
heat and protection.

They may also be grown in a fertile border
under glass. High humidity is important, and
sprinkling water on the greenhouse floor
('damping down') is a valuable aid to leaf and
flower production. Keep the tree well-watered and
once fruit starts to develop feed every week with a
fertilizer formulated for tomato plants. Success
entails tender loving care – you may need to
fertilize the early blooms by hand, for example –
but the rewards are mouth-watering.

The usual rootstocks are St Julien A, which is
semi-vigorous, 4.5m (15ft) high, and Pixy, 2–2.5m
(6–8ft) high, a dwarf stock that is good for
containers but requires very good growing
conditions. There are also genetic dwarf varieties,
even smaller, that make excellent pot plants.

'Peregrine', possibly the most widely grown, gives
   high yields in early August of large crimson-red
   fruits with juicy, flavoursome flesh.
'Rochester' is late-flowering and crops in mid-
   August, with medium-size fruits that are firm
   and juicy, yellow flesh and good flavour.
'Lord Napier', the most reliable nectarine for
   growing outdoors, fruits in early August. It is a
   yellow-skinned variety, with firm white flesh.

Other fruiting trees

There are many further kinds of tree fruits that
have a place in a productive garden, some of them
very ornamental, such as mulberries and quinces.
Chief among those you might like to consider are
figs, cherries and plums.

Netting protects the delicate flowers of Peach 'Rochester' against
damage from frosts.

Never prune stone fruits such as plums and cherries in winter, when open wounds increase the risk of silver leaf disease taking hold. Spring or summer pruning is best, because cuts then heal very quickly.

Figs

On first acquaintance, a fig tree might seem an undemanding candidate for the garden. It does not need a pollinator and so can be planted alone, nor does it need grafting on a rootstock. It is happy in almost any free-draining soil, pests and diseases generally leave it alone, and it is surprisingly hardy for a Mediterranean and Middle Eastern tree. However, if you want good crops of fruit you should take some preliminary precautions.

If left unrestricted for example, the greedy roots will feed and water an enormous tree, which will revel in freedom without producing a single fruit. The solution to this is to confine the roots by digging a planting hole 60cm (24in) deep and across, lining this with vertical paving slabs as a barrier to the roots' wandering tendencies. Spread broken bricks and pieces of shattered terracotta pots in the base of the hole, firmly packing these down to make a 25cm (10in) deep drainage layer, and then mix the excavated soil with a leavening of brick chunks or rubble, together with a handful of slow-release organic fertilizer such as bonemeal.

Planted firmly in these comparatively grudging conditions, the fig will be forced to fruit, especially if you guard against the frost threat by fan-training it on a south or south-west facing wall, and then protect the pea-size embryonic fruit over winter with horticultural fleece. Make sure the tree never dries out in summer.

Choice of variety for outdoor cultivation is usually limited in Britain to:

'Brown Turkey', a reliable hardy kind producing large purple-skinned fruit with red flesh and a rich sweet flavour in August and September.

'Brunswick' has large greenish-brown fruits in September, just as tasty but less prolific than 'Brown Turkey'.

'White Marseilles' fruits are large and pear-shaped, with flesh that is white or almost transparent, and finely flavoured.

Cherries

Cherries are either sweet (dessert) or sour (acid, pie or culinary). Although related, they behave differently as far as vigour and pruning are concerned. They can range in skin colour from butter yellow to deep purple, almost black. Acid varieties and some dessert kinds are self-fertile and may be grown alone, while the others need a pollinator that flowers at the same time and is also compatible – most nurseries will help you by recommending suitable partners.

To be sure of a good crop you need to net the fruit against birds, and this is one reason why the most popular method of growing cherries of all kinds is as a wall-trained fan, although you can also grow other small free-standing forms that are fairly easy to protect. Rootstocks are generally rather vigorous, producing very large trees, unless you choose the dwarfing stock 'Colt' or the even more restrictive 'Inmil', which limit their size to 4.5m (15ft) and 3.7m (12ft) respectively.

'Stella' is a dark red dessert cherry with large, sweet juicy fruits in late summer. It is self-fertile and also pollinates many other varieties.

'Morello' is the one acid or cooking cherry you are most likely to find. It is a relatively compact variety, which produces masses of deep red fruits in August.

'Merton Glory' has large, firm heart-shaped fruits with yellow, red-flushed skins, maturing in mid-summer. 'Morello' is an excellent pollinator for it.

A mature, fan-trained 'Morello' cherry tree in full bloom. This cooking variety is self-fertile so it can be grown alone.

Plums

Like cherries, plums are classified as dessert or culinary. Dessert or sweet plums are available in a range of colours from yellow through to purple, and are more susceptible to cold weather than the tougher culinary varieties, which are acidic and only edible when cooked. Varieties are generally grafted onto St Julien A rootstocks, which produces bushes up to 4.5m (15ft) tall, or Pixy, 2.4–3m (8–10ft) high.

Since plum flowers open early in the season, they are highly susceptible to frost damage. Covering flowering trees with horticultural fleece offers some protection, as does planting well away from sunny frost pockets. Plums are either mid-season or late-flowering, with the latter being a better choice for colder gardens – early-flowering varieties rarely succeed in British gardens. Although most popular plums are self-fertile, some do need a pollination partner and this must be selected from the same flowering group to ensure a good set.

'Victoria', a popular self-fertile dessert or culinary variety, it produces masses of large, pale red fruits with yellowish-green flesh, sometimes too many so that branches can break unless the fruits are thinned.

'Opal' is self-fertile and a delicious dessert plum with medium-size, red-skinned fruits with yellow flesh. It is ideal for harsher conditions.

'Czar' is the best-known culinary plum, robust and self-fertile, with oval deep purple fruits that are delicious when cooked and made into pies.

'Marjorie's Seedling' is a late variety flowering after the last frost, with the first fruits ripening at the end of summer. Self-fertile and dual-purpose, it produces masses of golden-fleshed fruit with purple skins.

Soft fruit

Soft fruit is invaluable in the garden. Shop-bought fruit, when available, cannot match the quality and taste of home-grown soft fruit. To get the best from the space allocated to soft fruit bushes, always buy certified stock. These are plants that have been inspected and passed as being free from pests and diseases, and are guaranteed to produce what it says in the description. Reputable retailers will always label stock as certified.

Planting soft fruits is best done in autumn through to early spring, provided the soil is in a workable condition (ie, not waterlogged or frozen). Once the plants are in production, you will have the added challenge of keeping the local bird population off the fruit. Cages around the fruit bushes are essential if you are to harvest any of the crop. They can be permanent structures – make them tall enough to enable you to walk around unbowed – or temporary coverings for crops such as strawberries. Ensure birds cannot get under the cages as they will both eat the fruit and may get tangled trying to escape.

Raspberries

These are accommodating plants that fruit well in partial shade, supremely well in full sun, and accept most soils, especially if these are fortified with organic matter – only waterlogged sites are unsuitable. Crops are available over a long season because there are both high-yielding summer varieties, fruiting on the previous season's shoots during June and August, and slightly less productive autumn kinds that crop on the current season's growth from mid September through to the first frosts. When buying raspberry canes, check they are certified as being virus-free. Raspberries are susceptible to many viruses, and sometimes canes from a fellow gardener or an anonymous source can be harbouring a virus that aphids might spread to your other plants.

Training Raspberries grow tall and are heavy when in fruit and need supporting to keep them neat and safe from wind damage. If you plan to grow just two or three plants, you can arrange them round the base of a stout post and tie them in with loops of string to keep them upright. Larger numbers are best grown along horizontal wires in rows dug 2m (6ft) apart, and with each plant spaced 45–60cm (18–24in) from the next in the row. The wires should be secured to posts with adjustable ring bolts to keep them stretched tight before the stems are spread out and tied in to the wires annually.

Pruning Autumn-fruiting varieties are easy to prune because they fruit on the current year's growth. In February all the canes are cut down to soil level, and the new growth is arranged on the wires and tied in as it appears.

Summer-fruiting raspberries produce the canes for next year's crop while this year's are still flowering and bearing, so you need to be more selective with your cuts. Once the harvest is over, cut all the canes that have fruited down to soil level. Select up to ten of the best new ones and tie these to the supporting wires.

Newly-planted canes need a slightly different treatment to encourage production of new canes. In the first spring after planting, cut each old cane down to soil level when you see new growth

To prevent damage from greedy birds, grow soft fruit in cages. The surrounding vegetables, however, are less tempting and will grow happily without this kind of protection.

appearing around its base. These young shoots soon develop into full-size canes, which you can tie to the wires and later prune according to variety.

Feeding Raspberries are both hungry and thirsty plants. In March sprinkle an organic, general fertilizer around their base and mulch with a 5cm (2in) layer of organic matter such as garden compost or well-rotted horse manure. Make sure you do this when the soil is wet, and the covering will then trap moisture in the soil, suppress weeds and keep the raspberry roots cool.

Summer-fruiting

'Glen Moy' has large, pale red fruits of good flavour over a fairly short season. Plants are spine-free and quite aphid-resistant.

'Malling Jewel', one of the tastiest summer varieties, has dark red fruits on compact plants that are very tolerant of virus infections.

'Malling Admiral', spine-free and high-yielding, produces bright red flavoursome fruit in mid July. Plants are vigorous and resistant to many common diseases.

'Joy' is a valuable variety, cropping heavily for a long season after many other summer kinds are exhausted. Its tasty dark red fruits are produced on very spiny stems.

Autumn-fruiting

'Zeva' is a popular autumn variety which is suitable for colder areas, with medium-size, dark red fruit from early September to the end of October.

'Autumn Bliss' has large, bright red fruits on strong self-supporting canes, and crops from late August until mid October.

Blackberries

One of the easiest soft fruits for gardens, blackberries produce trugfuls of fruit in return for minimal care and attention, provided you start with good quality canes and grow them in a sunny or partially shaded position. Plant in well-drained soil enriched with organic matter, spreading out the roots evenly in their planting holes, and firm well afterwards. Blackberries crop on long thick canes that grew the previous year, and often develop into large plants that need firm support and training on wires stretched between stout posts. After harvesting, prune down to ground level any canes that have borne fruit. Do not cut back the new, young canes, instead keep them and tie them in, but do remove any that appear weak or damaged at the base.

'Oregon Thornless' has unarmed canes and decorative divided foliage, with medium-size juicy berries of mild sweet flavour.

'Loch Ness', another thornless variety, is smaller – 2m (6ft) – than 'Oregon Thornless', and produces large berries in late August on stiff upright stems.

'Bedford Giant' is a traditional vigorous and thorny variety, 5m (18ft) or more in size, with fairly heavy crops of shiny sweet berries from early August to early September.

Colourful currants

Black, red and white currants are among the most productive fruits and need not occupy a lot of space, but they differ in their cultural routines.

Blackcurrants: These tolerate most soils, although they prefer organically rich sites in full sun, with some protection from frost because their early blooms can be damaged by low temperatures. They crop best on young stems produced the previous year, so an annual supply of new growth is vital. To ensure this, plant them deeply to encourage their underground buds to grow into vigorous, fruit-bearing shoots: the old soil mark at the base of the stem should be planted at least 15cm (6in) deeper. The plants should be positioned 1.5m (5ft) apart in rows 1.5m (5ft) apart. Pruning out one-third of all shoots each winter, starting with the oldest, also stimulates new growth.

'Ben More' flowers late, and is an excellent choice for colder gardens. Its fruits are large and refreshingly sharp, and borne in lavish quantities in late July.

'Ben Lomond' produces a heavy crop of large, plump, slightly acidic berries in late July. Plants are susceptible to mildew, but their compact growth is ideal for smaller fruit plots.

'Boskoop Giant' is a robust variety over 2.1m (7ft) high and bears lavish crops of sweet fruits in early July. Guard against late frost by covering flowering plants with horticultural fleece.

'Wellington XXX' is an old variety that is still worth growing. Its heavy crop of plump, sweet and juicy fruit ripens in mid July.

Red/white currants behave quite differently from blackcurrants, and are more like gooseberries in their cultural treatment. They form a permanent framework of stems that bear stubby fruiting sideshoots, and can be trained as fans or cordons or grown as bushes. Plant in any well-drained soil in a sunny position. If you are growing red or white currants as single bushes the plants should

be positioned 1.5m (5ft) apart in all directions; but if they are to be grown as cordons they should be spaced 45cm (18in) apart with 1.5m (5ft) between rows. Red and white currants (different forms of the same fruit) will produce heavy crops on plants that rarely exceed 2m (6ft), making them ideal for the smaller garden. Immediately after planting you need to cut back main shoots to half their length, sideshoots to just one or two buds long – fruits are then produced on the resulting short spurs.

'Laxton's No. 1' is a popular redcurrant variety, vigorous and prolific, juicy and well-flavoured.
'White Versailles', the best white currant, has long strings of sweet, pale yellow fruit.

Gooseberries

Often the only way to enjoy fresh gooseberries is to grow them yourself. They are sturdy, tireless plants that can crop well in partial shade, although their quality and flavour is best in a sunny position.

Plant bare-root varieties between November and March, container-grown plants any time in the year. Again, planting distances vary depending on how you grow the plants: place single bushes 1.5m (5ft) apart in all directions, but plant cordons 45cm (18in) apart with 1.5m (5ft) between rows. Immediately after planting, prune all sideshoots back to the main stem and shorten longer branches to half their length, cutting just above a bud. Prune fruiting plants in early winter by cutting new growth by half above a bud; then, in spring, trim sideshoots to 5cm (2in) and completely cut out any diseased or dead wood. Plants flower early and often set huge amounts of fruit, which may need thinning to improve size and quality. Do this when the berries are large enough for cooking, leaving the remaining fruits 5cm (2in) apart to continue developing.

Gooseberries are not greedy, but do benefit from a feed of organic fertilizer sprinkled round the base in April, followed by a 5cm (2in) mulch of organic matter such as well-rotted horse manure or home-made compost. Hand-weed rather than hoe plants, to avoid damaging their shallow roots, and keep them well-watered when the fruits are swelling.

'Careless' is a popular variety producing large, crisp berries in mid-July. It is a culinary variety that grows well in most soil types.
'Invicta' is a dual-purpose cooking/dessert variety, with large berries that are particularly tasty. Plants are resistant to mildew.
'Leveller', one of the best green-yellow varieties, produces extremely large berries, softly downy and oval in shape, in late July.
'Whinham's Industry' produces red gooseberries of excellent flavour, and is a good choice for growing in shade. The crop is produced in late July.

Strawberries

Probably the most popular soft fruit of all, strawberries are easy to grow and take up little room, producing delicious crops when freshly picked and still warm from the sun. Summer-fruiting varieties have the heaviest yields and largest fruit, maturing between May and August, while autumn-fruiting kinds – also called perpetual, ever-bearing or remontant strawberries – bear smaller fruit in June and again in early autumn, or heavier autumn crops if the first flush of blossom is removed.

Viruses can be a problem, causing a serious decline in health and yield, so make sure you start with healthy plants certified as virus-free. The best time to plant new strawberries is late summer, which allows roots plenty of time to become established before the soil cools. Choose a well-drained site in full sun for the earliest crops and add plenty of organic matter when preparing the ground. Dig a hole for each plant and form a small mound of soil in the centre, then position the new plant on the top of the mound and spread its roots evenly all round, down into the hole; check the base of the plant is level with the soil. Finally firm in place and water well.

Flavour is a contentious subject among strawberry growers. Both cultural practices and climatic factors can radically affect quality. Heavy rain a week before picking can dilute flavour, for example, whereas a hot dry summer with just enough irrigation to ensure survival, will remarkably concentrate the taste of the fruit. Autumn varieties seem to suffer less variation in flavour and can be relied on for good quality fruit after summer-fruiting kinds are finished.

Renewing plants Large-fruited strawberries have a limited productive life and quality deteriorates after 3–4 years, so you need to know how to propagate new plants as replacements. Select a healthy parent, one that isn't showing signs of virus disease (stunted or yellow-mottled leaves), and locate its runners – these are long string-like shoots running across the soil surface with small plantlets at intervals. Each of these will make a new plant.

These can be allowed to root into the ground where they lie, or you can root them into pots for easy transplanting or for growing in containers. Bury a 9cm (3in) pot in a hole under the plantlet and fill it with multipurpose compost. Using a bent piece of wire, secure the plantlet onto the surface of the compost. If kept moist, roots will usually have formed after a month and the plant can be severed from the parent runner for replanting elsewhere.

Strawberry beds Although a few plants can be grown as a group or short row, the traditional way to grow strawberries is in a dedicated bed of several parallel rows. Runners may be left to root in between, producing a carpet of fruiting plants: weeding can be difficult between the plants, but the overall yield from the area is high. A further benefit is that netting, feeding and watering is easier if all your plants are grown together.

Routine management is simple. When summer-fruiting varieties finish their crop, cut off all the leaves 10cm (4in) above the crown of the plants. Unless you need them for propagation, clear away the runners to keep the bed clean, tidy and under control. With autumn fruiting varieties, it is only necessary to clear away old or diseased leaves.

'Cambridge Favourite' remains the top choice for many gardeners, despite new summer varieties appearing annually. It is a reliable plant, with good crops of tasty medium-size, orange-red fruits in July.

'Pegasus' is a superior new variety with large, juicy red fruit that keep their attractive colour after harvest.

'Elsanta' is tops for flavour and produces masses of large, glossy orange-red fruits in July.

'Aromel', a classic and delicious autumn variety, yields irregular medium-size fruits from mid-July through to October.

'Rapella', another reliable perpetual, has heavy crops of well-flavoured bright red fruits in late summer and autumn.

Edibles in containers

If you are short of space, growing crops in containers is a productive alternative. Almost anything can be grown in a pot if it is large enough and you remember to water and feed regularly, and there is the advantage of being able to offer plants the most suitable kind of compost and perfect growing conditions. Many pests are easier to control, and you can extend the season by moving containers round the garden or indoors to follow the sun and protect plants from frost. In this way, you can even grow crops like potatoes completely out of season – if given the protection of a sheltered wall or greenhouse, potatoes planted in September will produce a delicious crop of small tubers just in time for the Christmas table.

Most types of fruit, including tree fruits if they are on very dwarfing rootstocks, succeed in containers, but perhaps the most obvious choice is strawberries, which thrive in the relatively small rooting space and are often beyond the reach of slugs and snails. Regular varieties do well in tubs, troughs and special strawberry barrels, with summer-fruiting kinds giving the heaviest crops. The best type for hanging baskets is the alpine strawberry, which has small, sweetly aromatic fruits from midsummer and all through autumn – 'Alexandra' is a classic variety, with tasty fruit around 1cm (½ in) long.

Herbs are superb hanging basket plants in the right position: you need to take care on exposed sites, where the wind can turn leaf edges brown and dry out compost. Strong sunshine all day can have the same result, so choose a sheltered bright position where the basket is in full sun for only part of the day. Do not over-plant baskets, because stressed herbs will often drop their leaves. Water every morning and evening in summer, and keep plants picked regularly. Most herb varieties are suitable, especially if you plant the taller or bushier kinds in the centre surrounded by an edging of prostrate pennyroyal, marjoram or some of the creeping thymes.

Edible hanging baskets

Garry Preston joined RHS Garden Rosemoor two years ago, armed with a wealth of gardening expertise, and now shares his valuable knowledge with the thousands of visitors who enjoy the gardens every year.

An allotment is the ideal place to grow a full range of vegetables, if you have the time and inclination. It is possible to grow a selection of kitchen produce in the back garden but not everyone has enough room. Where this is really limited, however, you can grow fresh vegetables in hanging baskets. All you need is spare wall space and a little know-how.

Garry's passion is container gardening, and he believes that with care almost anything can be grown in pots, and that 'all you need to grow vegetables is enough space for a hanging basket'. Tomatoes have long since been grown this way and there is no reason why you can't grow a wide range of other crops in hanging baskets too.

Planting an edible hanging basket

1 Fit the basket with a coir or fibre liner, and then spread this with a layer of plastic to help with water retention – pierce the plastic here and there to avoid water-logging. Quarter-fill with peat-free compost.

2 Cut a few holes in the sides and insert the tomato seedlings with their roots lying on the compost. Cover with more compost, add a few more plants, and continue the layers until the surface is 2.5cm (1in) below the rim. Alternatively, fill almost to the top and sow seeds at the recommended depth.

3 Water well and hang on a secure bracket, at first out of wind and strong sun to help plants settle in. Check daily and water before the compost dries out, and feed every week with seaweed extract from early summer until the crops are finished.

Garry's basket vegetables

In view of their limited capacity, it would be unrealistic to expect baskets to sustain the growth of tall, space-consuming crops like sweetcorn or Brussels sprouts, but there are plenty of other crops – vegetables, fruit and even edible flowers – that are perfect for them.

- **Tomatoes** Often the first choice for basket enthusiasts, the kind to choose are tumbling cherry varieties. Plants grow to about 30cm (12in) high, with semi-prostrate stems arching over the sides and laden with hundreds of juicy bite-size fruits. Good varieties are Balcony Red or Tumbling Toms, both available in yellow too.
- **Carrots** Their ferny foliage and sweet finger-size roots bursting with flavour make these a good dual-purpose choice. Choose stump- or round-rooted varieties, and sow them directly on the surface of the compost, because their roots easily break if you transplant them.
- **Strawberries** Summer, autumn and alpine varieties are all excellent and productive, with their fruits and long strings of runners trailing down the sides. Combine with curly parsley for a really decorative basket packed with flavour and vitality.
- **French beans** Without their tall cousins' need for support, these will bush out and arch magnificently from a hanging basket. Choose varieties with yellow pods for extra appeal and a drier regime.
- **Courgettes** These will make a mass of bold foliage, studded with large, yellow-orange flowers and succulent courgettes throughout summer. Sow in pots in a greenhouse or on a windowsill in April for planting as seedlings in May. Move the baskets outdoors in late May.
- **Spring onions** Simplicity itself in baskets because they take up very little root room. Sow direct in April for harvesting when stem bases are pencil thickness, and combine with loose-leaf lettuce for contrast.
- **Lettuce** Choose varieties that are also decorative – those with red or frilled leaves, for example – or with loose heads that can be repeatedly picked, a few leaves at a time. Sow in pots in a greenhouse or on a windowsill in March and transplant in April.

RHS KNOW-HOW

- Choose the biggest basket you can find. It will need very strong support, but you will be able to pack more produce in and it will be easier to look after because the large volume of compost dries out less rapidly.
- Use a sturdy bracket, because a full moist hanging basket is very heavy. Make sure it is fastened securely to the wall, using the right size screws and wall plugs inserted in holes drilled in the bricks, not the mortar joints.
- Avoid using sphagnum moss to line hanging baskets. Although it looks fresh and attractive, it may have been collected from wild plants, which are endangered in some places. There are several acceptable alternatives that are equally good-looking.
- Peat-free composts are excellent and comparatively light-weight, but some are difficult to moisten once they have dried out. Check for water requirements daily and twice a day in hot dry conditions. Remember that a dense leaf canopy or an overhanging roof may prevent rain from reaching the compost.
- For the tastiest healthy produce, always grow basket crops organically in peat-free compost. Avoid sprays with chemical insecticides, much of which could drift off overhead to land elsewhere. With care and vigilance, you should be able to pick or wash off any pests.

WATER

'Water adds movement to a garden and brings it to life.'

W ATER IS INTRINSIC TO LIFE itself, and more than any other single element has the power to alter the atmosphere of a garden and enhance the mood of the onlooker. A popular component of garden design for centuries, water gardening has become one of the most fashionable trends in modern gardens. It can provide a multi-sensory experience; visual enchantment aside, water introduces a wide range of sounds and valuable movement to the garden, and on a hot day it's hard to beat the pleasure of trailing a hand through cool water. Whether your penchant is for the formal tranquillity of a still pool, the thrill of cascading waterfalls, or a naturalistic wildlife pond, most gardens will be enhanced by the inclusion of a water feature.

The Royal Horticultural Society gardens are no exception, and their ample acres harness the stimulating, soothing and decorative qualities of water to full effect. The gardeners responsible for their upkeep are experts at maintaining the ecological balance and aesthetic appeal of a host of different water features. One of the highlights is a romantic stream which runs through the garden at Harlow Carr in Yorkshire. A streamside garden has been created on its banks, with an abundance of beautiful plants attracting and inspiring thousands of visitors every year. Setting up a new water feature can be daunting for the novice, but the failsafe advice of the RHS gardeners de-mystifies the process and makes water gardening accessible to all.

LEFT: The tranquil lake at RHS Garden Hyde Hall. ABOVE: *Iris Laevigata* 'Rose Queen'.

Water, in whatever form you choose, brings relaxation and tranquillity to a design and broadens the palette of plants that a gardener can grow. Water can also encourage the immigration of wildlife into a garden, with inherent benefits. (See masterclass on p94 for how to plan and build a pond.) A wildlife pond, with gently sloping sides, stocked with exuberant plants and fish, is irresistible to frogs – who eat slugs. Water can also encourage birds into a garden that in turn will reduce numbers of snails, slugs and aphids. It's always said that a pond needs to be in balance – not too much fertilizer and plenty of oxygen and plants – but water also helps balance the overall garden. Encourage wildlife into a garden and pest numbers will naturally fall. Water features also look and sound great from the smallest fountain or barrel pond to a much larger feature, and that has to be high on every gardener's list of priorities.

Choosing your water plants

For most gardeners, plants are the finishing touch to a water feature; they add colour and interest and can be used to create a statement in your design, or even to blend the water feature into the surrounding garden. There are four specific groups of water plants that offer a wide range of choice to create whatever effect you are trying to achieve, and which also serve their own beneficial purposes in or around the water. A properly functioning natural pond will benefit from incorporating three of the four types of water plants – deep-water aquatics, marginal plants and submerged oxygenators, with free-floating plants featuring as an additional option.

Rhododendron 'Pink Pearl' and *Iris pseudocorus* help the stream at RHS Garden Wisley blend into the overall garden design.

Deep-water aquatics grow in the deeper reaches of a pond. Their roots are submerged in the water, contained in baskets resting on the bottom of the pond, but their leaves float to the surface of the water. Leaves keep the water cool in bright conditions and provide shelter and shade for fish.

Marginal plants also have their roots submerged but hold their stems and flowers above the water surface. These plants blur the sharp boundaries from a garden to the pond and can look terrific throughout the year. They can also provide shelter for frogs and birds.

Submerged oxygenator plants have their roots and shoots under the water with flowers sometimes popping up through the surface of the water. They play a pivotal role in maintaining the balance of a pond. The leaves absorb carbon dioxide from the water – and produce small amounts of oxygen – ensuring wildlife, plants and fish can survive.

Free-floating plants have submerged roots and leaves that float on the surface of the water, which provide essential shade for fish and invertebrates. Many are invasive, but most die down in winter, sinking to the pond floor, and regrowing in spring.

Essential marginal plants

Marginal plants grow at the edge of a pond, with their roots in moist soil or shallow water and their topgrowth clearly visible. There are hundreds of marginal plants to choose from, all of them best planted in perforated baskets of aquatic compost lodged on shelves around a pond.

Acorus calamus (sweet flag) produces impressive 90cm (3ft) sword-shaped leaves, apple green and aromatic, with slightly crimped edges. Clumps grow to 90cm (3ft) across. 'Variegatus', more compact and suited to smaller ponds, has striking cream stripes and a red basal flush.

Butomus umbellatus (flowering rush) makes clumps 90cm (3ft) high and 50cm (20in) across. Beautiful bronze shoots grow up into olive green leaves, with summer rose-pink flowers on 1.2m (4ft) stems, perfect for adding structure to pond margins. If left unmanaged, the flowering capability of *Butomus umbellatus* declines, so divide it every two years to maintain vigour.

Caltha palustris (marsh marigold, kingcup) is a special sight in spring. Golden yellow flowers appear above mounds of shiny leaves. Plants grow 45cm (18in) tall and 15cm (6in) across. The variety *alba* produces white flowers on more compact plants.

Houttuynia cordata 'Chameleon' has multi-coloured leaves of red, green, pink and white and shapely small white summer flowers. It can be rampant, and can spread underground and pop up all round the pond. Plants grow 30cm (12in) high with an indefinite spread in damp soil.

Floating plants need a good depth of water to ensure their storage tubers and roots are not frozen in winter. A depth of 30cm (12in) is usually sufficient in an average British winter.

Lobelia cardinalis (cardinal flower) grows 90cm (3ft) high by 30cm (12in) wide, and produces spikes of scarlet flowers in late summer and autumn. Like most marginals, it is happy in any damp soil in the garden, but it may fall victim to slug attacks.

Mentha aquatica (water mint) has the potential to overrun a pond, but stays neat when grown in a basket and trimmed regularly. Its foliage is aromatic if crushed, while its spikes of tiny lavender flowers are produced in mid to late summer, attracting bees from far and wide. Plants grow 30cm (12in) high and will spread indefinitely.

Essential floating plants

Vital for providing shade for wildlife and for stabilizing temperatures in a pond, floating plants have roots that are permanently submerged in deeper water and foliage that floats at or near the pond surface. They are simple to plant – just throw them in the deep end, where they will sink to the bottom, form roots and send up their shoots.

Aponogeton distachyos (water hawthorn) needs a depth of at least 30cm (12in) and will spread strongly to 60cm (24in). Its evergreen leaves are oblong and often marked with purplish-brown blotches, while the white flowers, produced any time between spring and summer, smell seductively of vanilla.

Azolla filiculoides (fairy moss) has dainty fern-like leaves that quickly join together in dense mats. In late summer, the pale green foliage turns rich red and then often dies back in winter. Remove some plants in the autumn, and keep them frost free in a bucket of water until returning them to the pond in late spring. Thin the vigorous growth, and make sure it cannot escape into natural watercourses, where it can be invasive.

Eichhornia crassipes (water hyacinth) is noted for its gorgeous blue or lavender blooms, produced in spikes above the dark, swollen leaves and stems towards the end of a warm summer. Plants grow best in sunny positions and may be killed by severe cold, so it is advisable to take a few of the plants and overwinter them in a bucket of wet mud in a frost-free place. Re-introduce the following spring.

The flowers of *Aponogeton distachyos* fill the air around the pond at RHS Garden Wisley with a delicious vanilla scent.

Orontium aquaticum (golden club) is a placid
plant growing best in deep aquatic baskets in at
least 60cm (24in) of water – its blue-green
leaves will be erect rather than floating. The
intriguing flowers, like white pencils dipped in
burnished gold, are produced in late April and
stand 30cm (12in) above the water surface.

Pistia stratiotes (water lettuce) is a tender floater
which needs overwintering in a bucket of water
in a frost-free place. The reward for this care is a
charming colony of rosettes of downy, lettuce-
like foliage unlike any other water plant. Its fine
feathery roots are used by fish for spawning.

Stratiotes aloides (water soldier) adds intriguing
movement as its strong rosettes of spiky leaves
migrate from the depths to the surface at
flowering time. After its white July blooms die
back, the plants drop to the bottom and lie
dormant over winter. The leaves are sword-like,
green with white stripes and serrated, and rarely
stand more than 8cm (3in) above the water.

Ponds provide an extra environment suitable for a vast range of plants
that would otherwise be lost to a gardener.

Water lilies

Nymphaeas or water lilies are essential plants for
still water in open, sunny positions. There is a
wide choice of sizes and colours, both glamorous
and perfumed varieties. All require the same care.

Water lilies, regardless of size, are best planted
out in May into sunny positions in still water. Like
most water plants, water lilies are happiest in open-
sided pots or aquatic baskets lined with hessian
sacking. (Baskets and sacking are both available
from garden retailers.) The basket should then be
filled with aquatic compost – never use garden soil
as it will contain traces of fertilizer, along with pests
and weed seeds. Before planting, remove all the old
leaves and trim the roots by a third, then put the
new plant into the basket, ensuring that the top
2.5cm (1in) of stem is above the surface of the
compost. Top dress with grit as other aquatic plants

then lower the basket into the water on to bricks set at a height so that the leaves float on the surface. Leave the plant at this level until new leaves are produced and then lower it down until the new leaves are on the surface of the water. Gradually continue lowering the plant in this way until the basket is on the bottom of the pond.

When the plants are four years old they can be divided to make new plants. The process is quite simple and ensures healthy growth of the plant and is a cheap method of producing more plants if you have space for them! To divide them, lift the basket from the water and remove the plant from the compost. Cut through the thick roots, or rhizome, ensuring that each new piece of root has a shoot growing from it. Repot in aquatic compost and place in the water. Offsets are easily severed from parent plants, repotted and returned to the water.

Water lilies are stunning plants but you don't have to have a huge pond or lake like those at the RHS gardens in order to enjoy them, you can easily squeeze one of the smaller varieties into a more humble pond.

Small

This group includes varieties with flowers between 5cm and 15cm (2–6in) in diameter although the plants can spread up to 1.2m (4ft). They should be planted in water 15cm (6in) to 30cm (12in) deep.

LEFT TO RIGHT: *Nymphaea* 'Froebelii', *Nymphaea alba* and *Nymphaea* 'Marliacea Chromatella'.

Nymphaea candida produces white blooms with golden-yellow stamens. The cup-shaped flowers are held just above the water on stubby stalks.

N. 'Froebelii' produces masses of small, single wine-red flowers with dark orange stamens. Good for small ponds.

N. 'Graziella' bears numerous orange blooms with fiery red stamens. It has brown marbled leaves and flowers well in most ponds.

N. 'Laydekeri Purpurata' has deep pink blooms, with pointed petals and orange stamens.

N. 'Odorata Sulphurea' produces perky, rich sulphur-yellow flowers with pointed petals and brown-flecked leaves.

Medium

These flowers are 15–20cm (6–8in) across. The plants spread to 1.5m (5ft) and should be planted in water 30cm (12in) to 60cm (2ft) deep.

Nymphaea 'Gonnère' produces pure, snow-white blooms with rich golden centres, above compact layers of rounded mid-green leaves.

N. 'Masaniello' has speckled flowers with pale pink outer petals, deepening to rose red within. The stamens are a striking orange colour.

When replanting Iris laevigata, *cut the leaves down to 10cm (4in) high. This avoids the risk of newly-planted specimens rocking in the wind, and allows their roots to establish unchecked.*

N. 'Moorei' is a shy but gorgeous variety, with primrose-yellow blooms and yellow stamens.

N. 'René Gérard' produces star-shaped flowers with pointed petals in rosy-red. They are prolific when established.

N. 'William Falconer' is compact with deep port-wine blooms, marked in the centre with bright yellow. The young leaves are maroon.

Large

This is a vigorous and impressive group, bearing 20–30cm (8–12in) blooms. Plants can spread to 2m (7ft) and should be planted in water 60cm (2ft) to 1m (3ft) deep.

Nymphaea alba (white water lily) is ideal for large, deep ponds. Its white blooms have bright yellow stamens.

N. 'Charles de Meurville' is vigorous, with huge olive green leaves, wine-red flowers suffused with white, and orange stamens.

N. 'Fabiola' has pale green leaves and large blooms of deep pink, ageing to red.

N. 'Marliacea Carnea', prolific and fragrant, has blooms that vary between white and rose; most are soft pink with golden yellow stamens.

N. 'Marliacea Chromatella' is a good addition for natural ponds. It has coppery, purple-streaked foliage and primrose-yellow flowers with pointed petals.

Impressive pond irises

The iris family is extensive and includes many stately species and varieties that revel in boggy soil or shallow water. Any of these will instantly enhance the margins of a pond. Iris need their roots to be submerged in water, so planting should be done around the edge of a pond to a depth of up to 30cm (12in). Smaller growing varieties need less water depth. Cut back the leaves of newly-planted irises to 10cm (5in) and plant them firmly in baskets to reduce damage through wind rock – but don't plant them too deeply in aquatic baskets as aquatic compost will rot their stems.

As flower heads begin to fade, cut them out to prevent seed formation and depletion of the plant's energy. This will also stop any organic matter falling into the water, rotting and causing an imbalance in the pond. When the plants have finished flowering, lift and divide. Ensure that each new plant consists of a tuft of leaves and some rhizome with roots and buds which you can then return to the margins of your pond.

There is a huge range of irises, all in different colours and sizes, but here are a few favourites.

Iris laevigata is a native of Japan but equally at home beside British ponds. The slender plants grow to 90cm (3ft), producing green, sword-like leaves and purple-blue flowers with yellow base markings. 'Variegata' is similar but slightly smaller, with leaves edged in creamy white.

I. 'Snow Troll' reaches 75cm (30in) and produces elegant white flowers on tall stems.

I. *pseudacorus* (yellow flag), 90cm (3ft), is vigorous and colonizes many riverbanks in the wild, so is best reserved for large ponds. It bears stately spikes of prolific yellow flowers.

I. *versicolor* (blue flag) is a neat, tidy plant growing to 60cm (24in) and produces rich purple-blue flowers with white or yellow centres and mid-green leaves.

Planning a pond

With numerous ponds, a stream and a lake to care for, the gardeners at Harlow Carr are well versed in answering visitors' questions about water in the garden. For them, 'water adds movement to a garden and brings it to life'.

Water can add a magical element to any garden, whether in the form of a still shallow pool or sedate stream for quiet contemplation, or a splashing fountain or bubbling rill running through the plot to provide sound and movement. A simple pond is perhaps the most popular water feature and can range in size from a tub of miniature water lilies to an ornamental lake, depending on the scale of the garden.

Andrew Hart (Curator – right) and Matthew Light (Senior Supervisor, Estates – left) organize, plan and maintain the gardens and estates at Harlow Carr. For Andrew the outstanding joy of the job is 'planning for the future, and working with plants, features and people in a wonderful setting', while Matthew enjoys 'walking around first thing in the morning and appreciating the beauty of the gardens'. Both extol the water features there, for Harlow Carr has perfect examples of how water – whether ornamental or wildlife, still or moving – can be an essential and stunning component of the garden landscape.

For best results, delay turfing the edges of a new pond for up to a year. This allows the disturbed soil to settle and avoids hollows forming in the grassed areas.

Building a pond

1 Mark out the pond with sand, string, or a hosepipe – run warm water through it to make it pliable. Check the shape from all angles, and from above, before excavating the site. For a final depth of 60cm (2ft), dig the hole to 75cm (30in). Remove any roots and stones, and contour the shape to include steps, shelves and gently sloping sides.

2 Line the hole with a thick layer of old carpet, soft sand or inverted turf – this needs to be at least 5cm (2in) thick to prevent sharp stones from puncturing the pond liner. Spread the liner in place, tucking or folding it to fit over shelves and steps. Line wildlife ponds with a layer of soil or inverted turf on the bottom, and, if you want an ornamental look, after a year use more turves to disguise the edges of the liner.

3 If you are including a submersible pump, fit this now on a stand or brick to raise it above the pond bottom to prevent sludge being sucked in. Fill the pond using a hosepipe, adding the water very gently. This avoids churning up the soil and allows the weight of water to ease the liner into the contours. When full, add your plants.

Purple loosestrife *Lythrum virgatum* 'The Rocket' will brighten up any wet area around a pond, with its summer racemes of rose pink flowers soaring 80–90cm (32–36in) high from 45cm (18in) wide clumps of shapely foliage.

Stinking iris *Iris foetidissima* produces yellow-tinged purple flowers in early and midsummer, with the occasional pure yellow bloom. In wet soil it will reach 1m (3ft) high with an indefinite spread.

Marsh marigold *Caltha palustris* is a deciduous perennial for marginal and boggy sites, growing 60cm (24in) tall by 45cm (18in) wide and celebrating spring with an eye-catching display of bright yellow cup-shaped flowers.

RHS KNOW-HOW

- Introduce tench into ponds containing other fish species. Any sick fish will instinctively rub against the tench, sometimes called 'doctor' fish, and often recover within weeks.

- Include nooks, crannies and small bays in the outline of a natural pond to provide hiding places for wildlife, but avoid angular features and sharp edges, which will look out of place.

- Spread out any material cleared from an overgrown wildlife pond near the bank for a week to allow various aquatic creatures to return to the water. You can then transfer the debris to the compost heap, where it will rot down into a valuable organic soil supplement.

Planting deep-water plants

1 Line an aquatic basket with hessian or sacking then half-fill it with aquatic compost. Place the plant in the centre of the basket.

2 Fill in around the roots of the plant with more aquatic compost and firm it with your fingers to a level 2.5cm (1in) lower than the crown of the plant. Place a 2.5cm (1in) layer of grit on the surface of the compost.

3 It may be possible to lower the basket into a small pond from the side. For a large pond you will need help. Loop string through the corners of the basket. Take the string from two corners to the opposite side of the pond. Along with a friend, lower the basket into position. When it is in place, pull out the strings.

Allow a month for oxygen and chemical levels to stabilize

before adding fish to a new pond. Fish in wildlife ponds, though,

will eat the larvae of creatures you might want to encourage.

Tips from Harlow Carr

- Measure out your garden and plan the pond on paper, so that it neither dominates its surroundings nor is hard to find.
- Aim to build your pond in dappled light. If the site is too shady, plant growth will suffer; too bright and wildlife may shy away.
- Check the drainage of your garden, if necessary by digging a trial pit. A pond can act as a drainage point, with excessive rainfall causing the liner to lift or the water to overflow.
- Hire a detector to check the positions of buried pipes and cables before you start digging the pond site.
- Allow plenty of time for your pond project, and plan in advance where the excavated soil can go. If you have no spare room, neighbours may be glad of some good topsoil.

Liners

You can build your pond from any of these materials, each of which has particular qualities.

Butyl rubber Flexible and guaranteed to last for many years, this is the top choice for irregular-shaped ponds. It can eventually degrade in direct sunlight.

Rigid plastic Pre-formed and easy to fit, but you must ensure the liner is perfectly level and stable before filling it with water.

Concrete An excellent material for formal ponds and ideal for fish, especially if you use brickwork to build a sitting and viewing area at the edge.

Clay Great for wildlife ponds, this is installed by smearing and consolidating ('puddling') wet clay over the whole pond area. It must be kept submerged, because it cracks if allowed to dry out.

Andrew's favourite waterside pond plants.

Hostas *Hosta* 'Halcyon' has greyIsh-blue heart-shaped leaves in robust clumps 30cm (12in) high and 1m (3ft) wide. Dense clusters of violet-mauve flowers appear in summer on strong 45cm (18in) stems.

Primulas *Primula* Harlow Carr hybrids are beautiful Candelabras that thrive in the heavy clay flanking the stream that meanders through the gardens at Harlow Carr. Their flowers may be pink, orange, red, mauve and every shade in between.

Astilbes *Astilbe* 'Sprite' grows best in the moist margins around a pond or stream, where it develops into broad-leaved clumps, 50cm (20in) high with a 1m (3ft) spread, topped in summer by feathery panicles of tiny, shell pink flowers.

Never allow marginal plants to dry out. Keep them in a bucket of water while preparing their baskets, and water these immediately after planting. The best time for this is when pond plants are in growth, from spring to early autumn.

Planting pond plants

Whereas terrestrial plants usually require attention to drainage and regular supplies of compost and fertilizers, aquatic plants are grown by quite different cultural methods. Fertilizers, for example, can leach nutrients into a pond, which will upset its delicate chemical balance, encouraging undesirable algae to the detriment of preferred plantings and wildlife. Get the planting approach right at the outset, however, and the whole pond community will stabilize quickly and efficiently.

Pond plants are almost always grown for convenience in aquatic baskets, which have perforated mesh sides and are lined with hessian squares, readily available from garden retailers.

They are filled with loam or aquatic compost, which are not particularly high in soluble nutrients. Confining plants to baskets restricts the growth of possibly rampant species.

After planting, a 2.5cm (1in) layer of grit is spread over the surface of the compost to prevent fish and other pond creatures from foraging round the plants, disturbing the compost and clouding the pond water. The new plants are watered once and then the baskets are lowered gently on to shelves around the margins of the pond or into deeper water, depending on their preference. Any initial clouding in the water settles after a day.

The luxuriant growth of gunnera, hostas and polystichums are supported by readily available water around this pond at RHS Garden Rosemoor.

Wildlife and water

As described earlier in this chapter, incorporating a wildlife-friendly water feature in your garden can bring with it all sorts of benefits to the gardener, beyond an enjoyment of nature. Wherever your garden, in town or country, wild creatures will quickly find your pond, often within hours of filling. They are an important component of a healthy, balanced pond community and soon make themselves at home, especially if your pond is specifically intended for wildlife.

Designing for wildlife

To give your pond an instant 'natural' feel, create an informally-shaped pond using butyl liner. The pond can be whatever size you wish, or can accommodate, but the shape of it should be carefully planned with wildlife in mind. It is important to make the water feature as accessible to wildlife as possible, so ensure that there is a shallow beach area around the edge of the pond. This allows birds and small animals to safely gain access and exit from the pond. Pebbles are an ideal material for creating a beach. Do not cut grass around the edge of a wildlife pond, instead encourage it to grow long as it offers essential protection and breeding grounds to insects and animals. But remember to leave about one third of it clear of grass for observation – as you want to be able to see the wildlife haven you have created!

When digging the centre of the pond, make sure it is at least 60cm (2ft) at its deepest point. This provides protection for pond life in the winter, as shallow water freezes quickly in cold weather and will kill any wildlife near it. Before filling the pond

A well-balanced pond will attract a diverse range of wildlife, including dragonflies.

with water, you can add soil to a depth of at least 15cm (6in) as it creates a suitable substrate for plant roots and invertebrates. There are no aquatic plant restrictions in a wildlife pond – all types can be planted, and indeed they will ensure a good balance for wildlife. If you are a fan of fish, however, it is best to create another pond for them, as they are not beneficial in a wildlife pond; they eat many of the larvae that are essential for the pond.

Be prepared for some algal growth in wildlife ponds, but if the amount becomes unmanageable, scoop some out. (See p102.) Remember to leave any debris you remove from the water on the soil at one side of the pond for at least a few days. This gives any wildlife a chance to scurry back into the water.

Once you have filled your pond, sit back and watch for the arrival of some of these visitors.

The pond at RHS Garden Rosemoor is bursting with life in spring as the huge leaves of Gunnera manicata *unfurl to enormous proportions.*

Pond skaters are one of the first insects to find a new wildlife pond. The broad bases to their legs allow them to zip and dart across ponds, supported by the surface tension of the water.

Beetles soon arrive too, including water boatmen. These are flat, lozenge-shaped insects, grey-brown with darker undersides, that move or 'row' just beneath the surface. They kill young fish and aquatic creatures, but in turn can become food for larger fish, and therefore play an important part in balancing a pond.

Mayflies spend most of their time underwater, only surfacing to shed their skins and take their unsteady maiden flights. Fish feed with great voracity on the nymphs.

Dragonflies are beautiful creatures that lay their eggs on roots and shoots just below the surface of the water. Eggs soon hatch into nymphs, which may take up to five years to fully develop. In that time they are targets for birds and fish. At maturity a nymph climbs a plant stem, sheds its outer case and stretches out its wings to dry, ready for flight.

Snails sift through rotting detritus, filtering out harmful bacteria and reducing excessive organic matter, all of which helps maintain the health of a wildlife pond. If your aquatic snail population is too large, trap them by floating a lettuce leaf on the pond surface: next morning you will find many snails clinging to the underside.

Crested newts spend a lot of time in ponds, venturing out at night to hunt insects. The conspicuous spiky crest on the back of a male newt is stronger and harder in the spring mating season.

Frogs and toads devour slugs with enthusiasm, which makes them welcome allies in the fight against garden pests. Ponds provide areas for spawning and muddy margins are favourite overwintering refuges. Do not import frogspawn from another pond – frogs and toads will quickly find your pond by themselves.

Birds may be a blessing or a nuisance. Small ponds are welcome recreation and foraging areas for some birds, but herons and kingfishers can also be attracted if you keep fish and you may need to deter them in the interests of a balanced pond community.

Fish stocks

Fish add an extra dimension to ponds with their movement, colour and fascinating behaviour – some can even be trained to feed from your hand, although it is best to allow them to feed themselves and control the numbers of midge and mosquito larvae living in the pond. There is a wide selection of kinds to choose from, depending on the volume and depth of the water, ranging from wonderfully coloured koi, bursting with vitality if allowed plenty of room, to the many types of goldfish, whose ultimate size will match their living space.

Pond care

It is important to take care in the construction of your pond (see the masterclass on p94) and also to make sure it is placed in the optimum position – these early considerations will play a part in the amount of maintenance required to keep your pond healthy.

Removal of sharp stones, siting away from invasive tree roots and careful lining of your pond should ensure that structural repairs are unnecessary for a long period of time, but they might need to be carried out on occasion.

CLIMBERS

Climbers add a vital dimension to gardens. Grow them up any structure or allow them to scramble – they are invaluable.

CLIMBERS ARE AMONG THE MOST diverse and beautiful of all plants. Encompassing evergreen and deciduous types – some with excellent foliage, others festooned with flowers or studded with berries – there is a climbing plant for every situation. Most gardens will have numerous ready-made supports; walls, fences and established trees or large shrubs are all enhanced by the addition of a climber. Arches, tripods and obelisks, will provide alternative planting opportunities, creating height, structure and focal points throughout the garden. In the smaller garden it becomes vital to make the most of every available space, and the judicious use of climbing plants maximizes the potential of every vertical space.

With such a wide range of climbing plants on offer it can be hard to make an initial selection, or to know how to make the best of both new and established climbers so that they continue to look good and remain in the peak of condition. At each of the Royal Horticultural Society gardens, climbing plants of every imaginable type enhance the scene. From the humblest native ivy to delicate exotics, swags of clematis entwined with roses and curtains of intoxicating honeysuckle, the entire spectrum of these upwardly mobile members of the plant world are represented. All are tended by a dedicated group of expert gardeners. Follow their lead and you will be assured of outstanding colour, sumptuous perfume and frequently year-round appeal from some of the strongest performers in the garden.

LEFT: *Wisteria floribunda* 'Multijuga' trained onto a pergola. ABOVE: Autumn leaf of *Parthenocissus quinquefolia*.

In most gardens climbing plants are an effective way to add height to the display and make the most decorative use of upright surfaces. Covering walls and fences, from pillar to post, they can drip with blossom and very often look appealing all the year round. Each of the four RHS Gardens contains a superb selection of climbing plants, ranging from tough, hardworking kinds to the delicate and exotic.

How climbers climb

The fundamental difference between climbers and other types of plants is their ability to hoist themselves up above competitors in the search for light. Over aeons they have adapted to the situations in which they usually grow and evolved various ways of exploiting neighbouring plants and structures for support.

Some climbers need no help at all and are called self-clingers – the most familiar self-clinging plant is ivy, which attaches itself with aerial roots. Others produce adhesive pads that stick to supports, and a popular, vigorous example of this kind is Virginia creeper. Tendrils are leaves that have been modified into a useful way of grabbing hold of supports, as demonstrated by plants such as sweet peas and ornamental vines. In the case of clematis, the stalks of some leaves do all the hard work. Then there are twiners, whose whole stems twist and curl round supports to keep themselves upright as they grow: wisteria and bindweed are both supreme examples of twiners.

Many non-climbing shrubs grow well against walls, often secured into place to ensure even coverage and a neat display. Those that are not

reliably hardy benefit from some protection and are particularly suitable. Ceanothus, for example, looks wonderful trained on a sunny wall, it grows equally well as a self-supporting shrub in the open garden in mild areas but without wall protection may suffer frost damage in cold exposed sites. Forsythia is reliably hardy and another familiar example that is easy to train its bright yellow blooms making a brilliant display against a wall or fence.

Where to plant climbers

There are many potential sites that might accommodate a climbing plant or two in the garden. Climbers are the first and most obvious choice for clothing fences and walls, including the sides of the house, and some can cover large areas very quickly – choose the right kind, for example, and you could completely hide bland fence panels within a year. They are excellent sprawlers and smotherers, ideal for covering an old tree stump or pile of rubble, and often growing on to become localized ground-cover. An old tree stump enveloped by ivy, for instance, will turn into live green sculpture as well as becoming an excellent habitat for birds and invertebrates.

Climbers are perfect for disguising or enhancing more mundane elements of a garden. A washing line is essential to many households, but its posts can look stark and intrusive in an otherwise perfectly designed garden, so construct a tight tube of rigid netting around each pole, bury the bottom 15cm (6in) in the soil and plant climbers around the base. Pergola posts can also look bare without climbers, and need only be fitted with a few wires or staples to help climbing stems cover them with foliage and flowers. But make sure that the structure is strong enough to support the weight of the mature plant, as it can be considerable (for example, with wisteria or a vine). These supports should be checked regularly for safety's sake to ensure that they are sound.

Climbers look most natural when growing up informal hosts, such as old or large trees, whose limbs they will enliven with fresh growth – simply plant at the edge of the branch canopy of the tree, angle its stems towards the trunk and keep a close eye on watering until it is established. However, it is important to match a climber to its host plant – a vigorous climber may grow happily through the branches of large mature trees, but would swamp a small tree or shrub.

If you are growing a climber up the side of a building, be aware that most climbers are capable

Lonicera x tellmanniana is a deciduous summer flowering honeysuckle.

Protect slender clematis with clay drainpipes. Ease the topgrowth through a

60cm (24in) length of pipe immediately after planting. This keeps the base

of the plant cool and prevents damage from slugs and from hoes.

of scrambling under roofs and into gutters. Take note of eventual heights and spreads when planting a climber and then prune likely offenders to keep them under control. Watch out for the climbers for tough sites (p124), as these are naturally ebullient.

Equally, if climbers are neglected they can get out of control. If you want to try and renovate a plant, the best way to tackle the problem is to hard prune. Cut half of the stems down to 30cm (12in) above soil level. New shoots will regrow and when the plant is growing strongly, the remaining unruly stems can be hard pruned in the same manner. The brave alternative is to cut all the unruly shoots down to above ground level at the same time preferably in early spring. Most climbers will regrow after this treatment. (For more detailed pruning tips, see the masterclass on p112.)

How to plant a climber

Plants are usually supplied in deep containers, with their stems bundled for easy handling on slender canes and secured by means of green ties. It is best to plant the climber into well-prepared soil with these ties intact, to protect the stems from injury – once the plant is well firmed in and watered, the ties can be removed, allowing the shoots to be splayed out and retied to their permanent supports.

Climbers planted against a wall need special treatment. Dig the planting hole at least 45cm (18in) away from the wall. The soil at the foot of walls is in a rain-shadow and tends to be drier than the open ground, so by planting at this distance you will avoid the foundations and make sure sufficient water for healthy growth can reach

the roots. It is best to slope the rootball of the climber away from the wall, so encouraging roots to grow out into the open ground and increase the chances of quick establishment. The top growth can then be angled back towards the wall and the plant's supports.

Clematis grow best when their roots are in shade and their shoots in full sun; honeysuckle enjoys similar conditions. You can keep the roots cool by covering the area with an ornamental mulch of pebbles, gravel or grit. Plant clematis deeper in the soil than they were growing in their containers. This allows underground buds to develop and grow, forming stockier branching plants capable of surviving clematis wilt. Where possible, plant clematis at least 8cm (3in) deeper than the surrounding soil.

Watering is an essential aid to settling in the climber, so soak the ground after planting to ensure good soil and root contact and continue watering every week until you see signs of growth, indicated by new shoots.

Supporting climbers

Many species need help before they become established, even those which are eventually self-supporting. Raffia or string is always useful and can be looped around a stem, just above a bud, to encourage the plant to grow in the right direction. Twist ties, similar to those used for freezer bags, are ideal, as are wire rings, sometimes called sweet pea rings – these slip around both stem and support, eliminating any risk of plants slipping.

Whichever method you choose, it is vital that the ties are not too tight. This would restrict movement of water and nutrients through the

LEFT TO RIGHT: *Clematis* 'Jackmanii Rubra', *Clematis alpina* 'Frankie' and *Clematis cirrhosa* var. *balearica*.

plant or cause tears or rips in its stems, and there should always be room between the tie and the support for stems to expand. In practice you will rarely check every tie on a large climber, so it is wise to allow some slack from the start.

Climbers that are not self-clinging need to be attached to a support system of wires stretched at intervals across a wall. Drill and secure straining bolts at both ends of the wall, and join them with galvanized wire, which can then be stretched and tensioned between the bolts. Climbing shoots are secured to the wire with ties or twists.

Clematis all the year round

If the public were asked to name a familiar climber, there is a high probability it would be clematis, and if encouraged to narrow their answer to a single kind, the chances are it would be 'Nelly Moser'. For years this has been chosen by countless gardeners for its large mauve-pink and white striped blooms, but there is a host of other wonderful varieties that justify ranking clematis as Britain's favourite climbing plant. *Clematis montana* is another popular variety as it is a fast growing plant, often doubling its size in

the first year. This is the kind of climber to grow if you want rapid cover and flowers bursting through the tops of tree canopies in spring.

Spring-flowering varieties

When you see spring-flowering clematis in full bloom you know the growing year has started. All are pruning Group 1 (see page 111).

Clematis alpina 'Pink Flamingo' produces striking pink blooms in early spring. Plants grow about 3m (10ft) high.

Clematis alpina 'White Columbine' has pendent pure white flowers that are longer than other alpinas', and look stunning against the soft green foliage. Height 3m (10ft).

Clematis alpina 'Frankie' is a superb plant with short blooms of soft purple, and an unstinting display that can produce many hundred flowers consistently spring after spring. Height 3m (10ft).

Clematis macropetala 'Lagoon' is at its best in late spring when it produces deep-violet blue flowers of outstanding size and beauty. Height 5m (16ft).

Clematis macropetala 'Markham's Pink' produces strong pink blooms and is a dependable variety capable of growing 5m (16ft) high.

Clematis montana var. *sericea* has uniform, pure white blooms with yellow stamens in a gorgeous, lavish display. Plants easily reach 10m (32ft).

Clematis montana var. *rubens* 'Picton's Variety' has rounded, dark pink sepals. Blooms look and smell beautiful on plants growing 10m (32ft).

Summer-flowering varieties

Clematis that flower in summer look terrific either grown alone or complementing other summer-flowering plants.

Clematis 'Marie Boisselot' is a beautiful vigorous and large-flowered variety, producing 20cm (8in) pure white blooms with cream anthers. Height 4m (13ft). (Group 2.)

Clematis 'Ville de Lyon' flowers in mid summer, with flat, carmine red blooms and darker red edges. A sturdy plant, 3m (10ft) high. (Group 3.)

Clematis 'The President' has superb rich purple blooms from early summer to early autumn, on 3m (10ft) plants. (Group 2.)

Clematis 'Jackmanii Superba' has rich purple blooms from midsummer until autumn. White-flowered 'Jackmanii Alba' and red 'Jackmanii Rubra' are lovely, all 3m (10ft) high. (Group 3.)

Clematis 'Star of India' is a sumptuous plant. It has masses of blue-purple flowers, and a carmine-red stripe on each petal. Height 3m (10ft). (Group 3.)

Clematis 'Niobe' produces the richest, velvet red flowers of any clematis all summer long. Plants are 3m (10ft) tall. (Group 2.)

Autumn- and winter-flowering varieties

The show never stops as the autumn-flowering clematis take charge.

Clematis viticella 'Purpurea Plena Elegans' flowers in early autumn, with masses of ruffed lilac-purple sepals on 4m (13ft) plants. (Group 3.)

Clematis 'Margot Koster' has deep rose-pink blooms, 10cm (4in) in diameter, in early autumn. Plants grow to 4m (13ft). (Group 3.)

Clematis cirrhosa var. *balearica* is evergreen, with fern-shaped, bronze-tinged leaves. The pale yellow flowers, often spotted with red, appear in January and February. Height 3m (10ft).

Clematis groupings

Clematis belong to one of three groups, which were created for convenience to explain the differences in their routine pruning (see pruning masterclass on p114).

Group 1 Spring-flowering clematis bloom on stems which grew the previous year. These varieties are generally pruned after flowering, although some partial pruning can take place before flowering if a plant is weak and poorly shaped – some flowers are inevitably lost, of course, but the strength of the plant is increased.

Clematis macropetala spp. produces a stunning spring display on the previous year's stems and so falls into Group 1 for pruning.

Group 2 Late spring- and summer-flowering clematis bloom on stems produced in the current season. These are pruned in late winter to remove much of last year's growth. If left unchecked they will produce flowers, but mainly on the ends of long shoots and out of view.

Group 3 Summer- and autumn-flowering clematis bloom on both last year's and the current season's growth. About half of the shoots are pruned immediately after the first flush of flowers to maintain vigour and help produce stunning displays.

Pruning clematis

Bernard Boardman is a Supervisor in the Floral Department at RHS Garden Wisley, where he has worked for over fourteen years. During that time he has pruned thousands of plants, not a few of them clematis.

Of all the available garden climbers, clematis remain the firm favourite. But for many gardeners they are shrouded in mystery: plants will flower without much help – that is in their nature – but to get really superb results they have to be pruned, and pruned correctly, which is where the worries often start and doubts set in. Should a particular variety be pruned hard or lightly, before flowering or after? Ought it to be pruned at all? The gardeners at RHS Garden Wisley have the answers to these, and other misgivings.

Whenever Bernard is working in the garden or at shows, he can guarantee he will be asked by an anxious member of the public about the correct method of pruning clematis. He explains that method is one aspect, but just as important is the timing. He believes that 'When chosen and pruned carefully, clematis can provide colour all the year round', and that, if pruning is timed to perfection, you can help a clematis improve both vigour and flowering ability, whereas mistimed pruning results in a non-flowering plant and disappointment. For best results, do it the RHS Garden way.

Why prune?

The main purpose of the exercise is to stimulate a supreme display of flowers. In the process you will produce a shapely plant, keeping it within bounds and growing in the direction and style you want. Initially, cut out any diseased or dead plant tissues, which contributes to the overall health of the plant.

Then you can turn to the real art of pruning, but you need to know a little science first. At the end of

Clematis 'Comtesse de Bouchard'.

*The flower colour of a particular clematis variety can fluctuate
widely according to its growing conditions: it will intensify in
warmer conditions, but can noticeably fade in a very sunny position.*

each shoot is a terminal or 'apical' bud. This extends the length of the
shoot, but grows at the expense of lower ('lateral') buds. To make sure
these cannot grow and compete for nutrients, the apical bud produces
a chemical that inhibits their growth – this is called apical dominance.
Prune off the apical bud and you remove apical dominance with it,
allowing the lateral buds to grow and produce a bushier plant with
more sideshoots. Plenty of these means a lot more flowers.

That is the really essential science behind pruning, but before you
put theory into practice, you have to identify which kind of clematis
you are about to prune, because that will affect the timing of the work.

No pruning required

You can leave any clematis alone to flower naturally, often at the top
of lofty stems, and this is sometimes effective in wild gardens, but in
more orderly garden situations some degree of control is essential to
create the most lavish results. Winter-flowering clematis species and
varieties are often deliberately excepted from the usual pruning rules,
though. They may have evergreen leaves and gorgeous spotted
flowers that can adorn walls and fences any time from December to
early March – *Clematis cirrhosa*, with its bell-shaped cream flowers
and red flecks, is a typical example. These do not need pruning at all
unless stems begin growing into areas where you do not want them.
If this is the case, prune immediately after flowering.

Pruning for growth

All clematis should be pruned after planting to a lower pair of strong
healthy buds. Although this might appear wasteful, it gives plants an
incentive to grow energetically and can be more productive in the
long run as it will encourage basal shoots to grow and create a
strong, low-branching framework that will be festooned with
flowers. Established plants are pruned according to their group.

Bernard's favourite clematis

'Comtesse de Bouchard' is a
strong plant, pruned as a group 3
variety. It has masses of large,
bright mauve-pink flowers in
summer. Plants grow to 3m (10ft)
with a 90cm (3ft) spread.

'Guernsey Cream' flowers early
and needs group 2 pruning. The
flowers are 5cm (2in) across and
creamy yellow. A second flush, this
time white, is sometimes produced
later. Plants prefer semi-shade and
grow 3m (10ft) high by 90cm (3ft)
across.

'Jackmanii' (above) is a vigorous
plant with a group 3 pruning
routine. In midsummer it is
smothered with masses of velvety,
dark-purple blooms. Plants grow
3m (10ft) high and 90cm (3ft) wide.

Which group?

Popular clematis found in most garden centres and nurseries can be allocated to one of the three pruning groups.

Group 1 *Clematis alpina*; *C. alpina* 'Frances Rivis'; *C. macropetala*; *C. montana.*

Group 2 *Clematis* Anna Louise; *C.* Arctic Queen; *C.* 'Bees' Jubilee'; *C.* Blue Moon; *C.* 'Carnaby'; *C.* 'Daniel Deronda'; *C.* 'Doctor Ruppel'; *C.* 'Duchess of Edinburgh'; *C.* 'Elsa Spath'; *C.* 'Guernsey Cream'; *C.* Josephine; *C.* 'Lasurstern'; *C.* 'Miss Bateman'; *C.* 'Nelly Moser' (above); *C.* 'Niobe'; *C.* 'The President'; *C.* 'Vyvyan Pennell'; *C.* 'William Kennett'.

Group 3 *Clematis* 'Abundance'; *C.* 'Bill MacKenzie'; *C.* 'Comtesse de Bouchard'; *C.* 'Duchess of Albany'; *C.* 'Ernest Markham'; *C.* 'Gipsy Queen'; *C.* 'Hagley Hybrid'; *C.* 'Jackmanii'; *C.* 'Rouge Cardinal'; *C.* 'Star of India'; *C. tangutica*; *C.* 'Ville de Lyon'.

Group 1

Late winter If plant growth is weak, prune all shoots from the previous year by half their length, always cutting to a strong pair of buds. Mulch plants with well-rotted manure, leaf mould or compost.

Late spring Train and tie in all new growth to appropriate supports. Lower shoots that have finished flowering already can be cut back to a pair of strong buds.

Early summer All shoots that have flowered are pruned back to one pair of buds from the main framework of the plant.

Group 2

Summer After the initial trim following planting, new growth will be branching from near the base, and this needs to be tied into appropriate supports. Some flowers may appear in this first year.

Late winter On each main shoot, cut back all growth to the lowest pair of strong buds. Mulch plants with well-rotted manure, leaf mould or compost.

Summer Continue tying in growth to create a strong framework. The plant will produce a spectacular display of top quality blooms on shoots that will be pruned next winter. Continue this cycle of pruning, mulching and flowering.

Group 3

Summer After the initial cut back, the plant will produce new branches from near its base and these need tying in. Some flowers may appear in this first year.

Late winter Cut back all the previous year's shoots by half their length, always pruning above a strong pair of buds. Mulch plants with well-rotted manure, leaf mould or compost.

Summer Immediately after flowering, cut half of the shoots to 30cm (12in) above soil level, and leave the rest unpruned. Water and feed with a balanced fertilizer.

Key pruning stages

1 Train and tie in new clematis shoots to appropriate supports – either wires, trellis or posts. When tying in you should aim to create a well-spaced, attractive framework which will ensure a healthy plant, by creating good air circulation, and will produce flowers over a larger area.

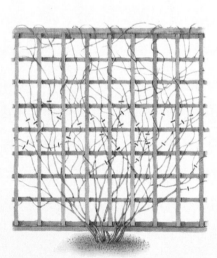

2 When pruning a clematis shoot by half its length, always make sure that you prune back to above a strong pair of buds.

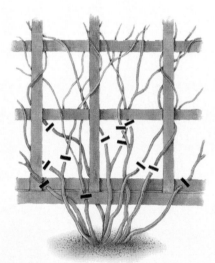

3 If you are pruning a clematis shoot harder than half way down, cut back to the lowest buds, making sure they are a strong, plump pair.

RHS KNOW-HOW

- Clematis are thirsty plants and develop deep root systems in their search for water, but they cannot tolerate waterlogged conditions. Enriching the soil with organic matter at planting time will help it to retain water while also improving drainage.

- Make sure support wires are securely connected to their posts or bolts, and keep them well tensioned. As plants grow, they become heavy and exert pressure on a wire, causing it to bow if it is slack.

- Instead of pruning everything for a neat tidy finish, leave some flowers to develop seed heads. These are often attractive to both gardeners and wildlife, and may offer a free source of seeds for new plants.

- Clean healthy prunings should be shredded or chopped into smaller pieces before putting them on the compost heap – smaller fragments rot down quickly, especially if mixed with soft green material like weeds or lawn mowings. But never add diseased prunings to the heap.

- Only prune when you have the time and won't rush the job. Allow yourself plenty of opportunity to step back and assess progress. Many plants have an amazing ability to recover after being hard pruned, but generally it is better to remove too little rather than too much. Never cut anything off without a good reason.

Glorious wisterias

There is no more breathtaking sight in May and June than a mature wisteria in full bloom. The pendent chains of flowers come in shades of mauve, blue, pink or white, and last until the summer heat begins to build. Many visitors to the RHS Gardens ask how they can improve the performance of their wisterias, with non-flowering being perhaps the most frequent complaint. To get the most prolific flower display and growth from a wisteria, it is best to start at the beginning.

Plants grown from seed never flower as strongly or as quickly as grafted plants, so always check the stem of a new plant to see if it has a raised grafting

Wisteria floribunda 'Alba' is a beautiful sight when in full bloom.

point. Grafted plants grow more strongly and produce flowers when they are three or four years old. They should be planted in soil enriched with large amounts of organic matter such as compost or well-rotted manure. Wisterias are thirsty, as well as hungry, and must never be allowed to dry out in spring or summer, particularly during their early formative years. Finally, all varieties need a sunny position, ideally against a south-facing wall: shaded plants do not flower.

After a three-year honeymoon period, during which a new wisteria builds up strength and structure, pruning can start, and how you do this is often critical for good flowering. The first trim is in summer, after flowering ends or in August for non-bloomers, and involves cutting sideshoots to leave six pairs of leaves – this shortens them to about 30cm (12in) long. Prune again in winter, further shortening these sideshoots to three pairs of buds or about 15cm (6in) long. Always cut 2.5cm (1in) above a bud as these are easily damaged by clumsy pruning. This dual pruning in summer and again in winter is important in the early years because an untrimmed young wisteria may romp into a large plant without producing a single flower. All wisteria flower buds can be damaged by late frosts, when they will shrivel up and stay tightly closed, making plants look barren.

There are many wisteria varieties to choose from, all of them capable of transforming a warm wall into a cascade of lovely colour.

Wisteria floribunda (Japanese wisteria) is a superb climber reaching 4m (13ft), with fragrant bluish-purple flowers on slender racemes that open from the bottom upwards.

The foliage on non-flowering and flowering shoots of ivy are often different in shape. Fruits in autumn follow the inconspicuous green flowers, which provide a late source of nectar and are popular with birds.

Wisteria floribunda 'Alba' has white flowers with a lilac tint, in racemes up to 60cm (24in) long.

Wisteria floribunda 'Multijuga' is very fragrant, with lilac blooms on racemes that can reach 90cm (3ft).

Wisteria floribunda 'Violacea Plena' is a lavish violet-blue variety with scented double flowers.

Wisteria sinensis (Chinese wisteria) is more vigorous, up to 18m (60ft) tall, with deep lilac flowers in racemes 30cm (12in) long. There are several fine varieties.

Wisteria × formosa 'Yae-kokuryû' is vigorous, up to 10m (30ft), with sumptuous double blooms with rosettes of deep purple petals.

Wisteria brachybotrys 'Shiro-kapitan' is a strong plant, growing 10m (32ft) in favourable conditions. Its lightly-scented flowers are white, in 15cm (6in) racemes.

The truth about ivy

Ivy is a willing climber with sometimes rampant growth that can totally cover a wall or tree. Its self-clinging aerial roots are often blamed for damaging walls, but it is quite safe for planting on a sound wall and will only disturb loose flaky mortar or brickwork that is already crumbling. Nor does ivy strangle healthy trees. It will use them to support its upward progress and will sometimes completely smother a dead tree trunk, but it is innocent of any lethal intent and its heavy canopy of growth will only cause the collapse of an already weak tree that is exposed to wind.

Growing ivy is relatively easy in most gardens, because the plants thrive in almost any soil. Green varieties grow happily in shade or sun, but those with variegated leaves need a sunny position to sustain their colouring. The pruning regime is uncomplicated and involves simply cutting shoots back wherever they are getting out of hand – growing into gutters, for example, or across paths. Ivy tolerates hard pruning, and usually grows back with renewed vigour.

Ivy is a large and diverse family with a confusion of common names that often indicate the plant's origin. Common ivy, *Hedera helix*, is the native species of British hedgerows, but there are also Persian ivy (*H. colchica*), Canary Island ivy (*H. canariensis*), Irish ivy (*H. hibernica*), Japanese ivy (*H. rhombea*) and Himalayan ivy (*H. nepalensis*). *Hedera helix* f. *poetarum* is known as Italian or, just to be different, Poet's ivy.

Hedera colchica is most commonly seen, with large plain green leaves, and its yellow-variegated form 'Dentata Variegata', but there are many other, often more glamorous ivies that deserve to be grown.

Hedera colchica 'Sulphur Heart' has yellow markings merging into a mottled pale and dark green background. Unrestrained plants can reach 6m (20ft).

Hedera helix 'Oro di Bogliasco' ('Goldheart') is eye-catching, with large central splashes of yellow on mid-green leaves. Slower growing than other kinds, up to 6m (20ft) high.

Hedera helix 'Ivalace' is compact with closely arranged foliage. Each leaf is bright green and curled at the edge. Plants reach 2m (6ft) high.

Hedera maderensis produces broad, glossy green leaves with pink stalks that turn a copper colour in winter. Plants grow 4m (13ft) high.

Honeysuckles

These are some of the easiest climbers to grow. Undemanding, generous with their flowers and quick to cover fences, trees and other supports, they need minimal attention to ensure an extra special show. These plants are happy in sun or partial shade, but make sure you add plenty of organic matter to well-drained soil. Don't let honeysuckle dry out in a hot summer, or become waterlogged, and only prune to restrain excess growth, cutting out whole shoots after flowering.

Lonicera periclymenum is the native British common honeysuckle or woodbine. The perfume from a stretch of hedgerow hosting this beautiful, vigorous climber is unsurpassed, and *Lonicera periclymenum* 'Graham Thomas' is a superb variety with fragrant white flowers that age to yellow. Plants grow to 8m (26ft) and look sensational in full bloom.

Lonicera × americana is rampant and can reach 10m (32ft). Its fragrant purple-tinged blooms open white, fading to cream and then yellow.

Lonicera × brownii 'Dropmore Scarlet' is a popular choice for its small, fragrant orange-red flowers. Plants grow to around 5m (16ft).

Lonicera henryi, evergreen in mild locations, has soft downy shoots that bear yellow flowers, blushed red, in summer. Height 4m (13ft).

Lonicera japonica 'Halliana' is very fragrant and pure white, fading to yellow. Plants can retain leaves in mild winters, and grow to 10m (32ft).

Lonicera × tellmanniana is a wonderful plant with rich, coppery orange blooms all summer. Plants grow to 5m (16ft) high.

Sweet peas and Chilean glory flowers are hungry climbers. Nip off fading blooms and feed regularly with a fertilizer high in potash, such as one formulated for tomatoes, to encourage plenty of flowers.

Annual climbers from seed

These are climbers that complete their life cycle in a year and are raised from seeds sown in spring. They flower all summer, often setting their own seeds which you can harvest in autumn and winter from the exhausted plants.

Lathyrus odoratus (Sweet peas) are easy to grow and produce a colourful display of flowers in summer, many sweetly-scented and excellent for cutting. Fragrant varieties include 'Anniversary', white; 'Firecrest', orange-red; and 'King Size Navy Blue', very dark blue. One of the first sweet peas to be grown in Britain, 'Matucana' is a tall variety with deep blue flowers with purple wings and a bewitching perfume. The full range is immense, with some tall kinds growing over 2m (6ft) while others stay dwarf and suitable for containers. All require full sun, well-drained soil and plenty of organic matter at sowing or planting time. Seeds can be started indoors during autumn for overwintering in a cold frame and planting out in March, or you can sow them directly outdoors in March for later flowers.

Eccremocarpus scaber (Chilean glory flower) has an exotic appearance and quickly covers fences and walls to a height of 3m (12ft). In summer, it bears clusters of tubular orange, red or pink flowers. The plants are frost-tender, so sow seeds in February in a heated propagator and do not plant out until danger of frost has passed. In autumn you can dig up the plants and overwinter them in a heated greenhouse. Plants do self-sow occasionally though, especially when grown in very well-drained soil and full sun.

Cobaea scandens (Cup and saucer plant) can be rampant and is an ideal choice for quickly covering a large fence. Often reaching 4m (13ft) in a season, its large bell- or cup-like flowers are basically purple, occasionally white, and last well into autumn; in mild areas, plants can survive the winter. Seeds are sown individually in pots in February, and the resulting seedlings planted out in June, after hardening off, in well-drained soil and a sunny site. Avoid sites where plants can dry out or sit in waterlogged soil – both conditions will result in lack of flowers.

Thunbergia alata (Black-eyed Susan) is a lovely little climber that easily scrambles up wigwams of bamboo canes in large containers. It grows best in mild areas and in sheltered positions. Flowers appear all summer and can be orange, cream or white, always with a distinct black centre. Soak seeds overnight and sow in threes in 9cm (3in) pots of multipurpose compost. Harden off and plant outside in late May, ideally in the shelter of a south-facing wall. Plants can be overwintered in a heated greenhouse.

Ipomoea (Morning glory) is available in a range of colours. *Ipomoea purpurea* 'Heavenly Blue' is a very popular choice, but 'Scarlet O'Hara' has scarlet blooms, each with a white throat. Soak seeds overnight in early April and sow individually in 9cm (3in) pots of multipurpose compost, kept in a warm propagator. Harden off seedlings in May and plant out in June. Warmth is the key to success, and plants that get too cold will turn yellow, especially during the first few weeks of growth. When grown well, flowering plants are an arresting sight climbing up walls, fences and supports.

Scented climbers

These are great favourites and ideal for positioning near a door or pathway, or close to opening windows where their fragrance can be enjoyed from inside too. They are also excellent for pergolas and archways – in fact anywhere that is likely to be passed regularly so that their special qualities are easy to appreciate. In addition to the plants listed below, don't forget to consider scented honeysuckles (p118) and wisterias (p116) as well as the roses suggested on p115.

Clematis armandii is a super year-round plant, glossy green leaves and subtley-scented, white flowers from January through to April. It can be slow to become established but once it has done so, it will happily fill a fence or scramble through shrubs adding invaluable winter interest.

Jasminum officinale (common white jasmine) is a strong climber that can reach 8m (26ft), and produces simple, white trumpet-shaped flowers in clusters from early summer to early autumn if planted in well-drained soil in a warm sheltered spot. A south-facing wall is perfect because the bricks reflect heat during the day and retain some stored up to radiate at night. The delicious lingering scent of the blooms makes extra attention to the plants' welfare worth every effort – if really happy, plants will retain their leaves over winter.

Trachelospermum jasminoides is an outstanding slow-growing climber that will eventually reach 10m (32ft) high if supplied with good drainage and a sheltered position against a warm wall. Its small flowers are white, fading to cream, with a concentrated sweet fragrance. The oval leaves of dark polished green are evergreen, but appreciate a little protection in a severe winter against wind- and frost-scorch.

Climbers for foliage

Whereas the leaves of some climbers are comparatively plain, others have such wonderful foliage that they deserve planting in a prominent position where they can be admired, covering

Jasminum officinale is a beautiful fragrant addition to any garden.

something you would rather not see – an ugly fence or building – or as a foil to other complementary flowers. Evergreens, like ivies (p117), also supply valuable colour and signs of life during winter.

Actinidia kolomikta is fascinating, with the leaves of older shoots on established plants divided into a green upper portion, while the lower segment is strikingly mottled with pink or white. Young plants growing at your local nursery are unlikely to show the full colour combination, but if planted in well-drained soil, with full sun to ripen the stems, the distinctive motley colouring will soon appear. A graceful highlight for a wall or fence, it grows 4m (13ft) high.

Humulus lupulus 'Aureus' has fresh yellow foliage and pendant spikes of greenish-yellow female flowers or hops. The leaves are bold and will smother an eyesore within a couple of months. It is best grown in full sun and well-drained soil that does not dry out in summer. Plants grow quickly to 6m (20ft), but die right down in winter, reappearing early the following spring.

Smilax aspera is evergreen in mild areas of Britain and has some of the best foliage in the garden, with heart-shaped leaves that are glossy green and look and feel leathery. The spiny stems scramble through trees and over walls, and look particularly effective lolling over an old tree stump. In well-drained soil and a sunny position, plants grow quickly to about 4m (13ft) high.

Climbers for spring

It may be flowers, it could be foliage, but some climbers are just irresistible in spring.

Akebia × pentaphylla is perfect for draping over an old tree, where its chocolate-scented blooms fill the spring air with their perfume. Two kinds of flower grow on the same plant: male flowers are small and produced at the end of each flower spike, while the large female blooms develop at its base. A marvellous under-rated climber that keeps its elegant leaves in mild winters and grows about 10m (32ft) high.

Akebia quinata (chocolate vine) is more familiar, and popular for its vanilla-scented, brownish-purple spring flowers. Both this and its cousin *Akebia × pentaphylla* grow well in any soil in full sun. Be patient with newly planted specimens because they can take a year or two to establish, after which growth can be rapid. Height 12m (40ft).

Solanum crispum 'Glasnevin' has devastatingly blue flowers that are beloved of many gardeners.

Ercilla volubilis is a self-clinging evergreen for a sheltered spot, where it will produce dense spikes of purplish-white flowers in spring, occasionally followed by purple berries. Its dense gleaming foliage is made up of attractive oval leathery leaves. Plants grow to 10m (32ft) in partial shade and any well-drained soil.

Schisandra rubriflora is invaluable for covering a fence or wall. Deep crimson flowers are produced on pendulous stalks in late spring against a background of toothed leathery leaves, deep green with paler undersides. Grow in sun or partial shade, in any well-drained soil that is enriched with organic matter. 8m (26ft).

Climbers for summer

Warm, dry conditions bring out the best in many climbers; flowers abound and the foliage is fresh and easy. Summer is a wonderful season for climbing plants.

Campsis grandiflora (Chinese trumpet vine) is magnificent, with an altogether exotic appearance. Its flowers are its glory – trumpet-shaped, up to 8cm (3in) long and deep glowing orange-red, all gathered in lax drooping clusters during late summer. In the coldest areas it needs the shelter of a south-facing wall, but elsewhere it is surprisingly hardy if grown in sun with very good drainage. Height 6m (20ft).

Campsis × tagliabuana 'Madame Galen' is similar in habit and cultivation to *Campsis grandiflora*, but with masses of brilliant salmon-red blooms and a downy underside to its leaves. Provide strong support for the vigorous growth.

Lathyrus latifolius, the everlasting or perennial pea, is a herbaceous climber, so it dies down and remains dormant every winter, reviving again in spring year after year. Small racemes of brilliant mauve or purple flowers are produced in summer and early autumn. Plants grow to 2m (6ft), and thrive in sunny positions and well-drained soils.

Schizophragma integrifolium has deep green, coarsely-toothed oval leaves and flattened flowerheads, up to 30cm (12in) across and composed of white bracts 9cm (4in) long, arranged in a conspicuous ring around the clusters of tiny fertile flowers. An ideal climber for north-facing walls on any soil, its growth is slow for the first two years but eventually reaches 12m (40ft).

Solanum crispum 'Glasnevin' (potato vine, perennial nightshade) is a vigorous favourite with downy leaves and flowers similar in shape to those of the potato, but much more colourful, in a rich shade of purple-blue with bright yellow centres. They are slightly fragrant too, and are produced for most of the summer months. Grow in full sun. Plants can reach 5m (16ft) high.

Tropaeolum speciosum (Scottish flame flower) is a choice perennial for planting to scramble through hedgerows and up trees, as well as on fences. Its bright scarlet nasturtium flowers appear in summer and contrast dramatically with the blue-green leaves. Roots must be shaded and shoots grow best in full sun, losing their leaves in winter but reviving in spring. Height 3m (10ft).

Climbers for autumn and winter

Even as the sun weakens, some climbers come into their own. There is no excuse for bare walls or pergolas with this selection of stunning climbers.

Celastrus orbiculatus (oriental bittersweet, staff vine) produces tiny green flowers in summer, followed by black fruit in autumn where male and female plants are grown together. The fruits ripen slowly, eventually bursting open to reveal yellow flesh and bright red seeds. The green foliage turns clear yellow as temperatures start to fall in autumn. It is a strong-growing, unfussy plant growing 15m (50ft) high in sun or partial shade.

Parthenocissus quinquefolia is commonly – and correctly – called Virginia creeper. But so too can be P. tricuspidata, instead of the correct Boston ivy. Common names vary in different parts of the world, but a botanical name is always the same.

Parthenocissus tricuspidata (Boston ivy) is a common sight in many gardens, and for very good reason. Its autumn colour is majestic, as the handsome lobed leaves turn from green to rich crimson and scarlet. Plant in partial shade against a high wall, where the self-clinging tendrils will easily hoist stems to 20m (65ft).

Pileostegia viburnoides is a superb evergreen for every kind of soil and walls with any aspect, including shady and north-facing. It is slow to get established, but once happy can cover a wall 6m (20ft) high with its slender leathery foliage and dense heads of fluffy white or cream flowers in early autumn.

Vitis coignetiae (crimson glory vine) uses tendrils to cling to supports, often romping high into trees 15m (50ft) tall, where it is a spectacular sight in autumn as its large dark green leaves turn various shades of vivid red, scarlet and orange, all jostling for appreciation as the nights draw in. Plants prefer partial shade and soil low in organic matter, because slight stress produces a brighter and longer autumn display.

Climbers for tough sites

Some positions are less hospitable than others, but there are climbers capable of thriving in the face of adversity.

Fallopia baldschuanica (Russian vine) is possibly the toughest climber on the block, producing a rampant irrepressible tangle of growth 15m (50ft) or more high within a couple of years and covering everything in its path. The white flowers, produced in summer and autumn, are lovely and create a foaming mass of blooms for weeks on end. Plants grow well in sun or partial shade and any soil type, and are ideal for screening and disguising eyesores. But think carefully before you plant this vine – make sure you have enough space for it to scramble happily without frequent pruning, otherwise it could become a maintenance nightmare.

Hydrangea anomala subsp. *petiolaris* (climbing hydrangea) is rugged and happy to grow on a north-facing wall or similar bleak shady site. Very slow to start, plants can reach 15m (50ft) once established, and produce masses of flattened white flower heads in summer. Any soil type is acceptable. Help plants cling to supports until they are capable of doing it themselves with their aerial roots.

Parthenocissus quinquefolia (Virginia creeper) is a self-clinging climber capable of growing 15m (50ft) high. Its large leaves, made up of stalked leaflets, turn from matt green to vibrant orange and red in autumn. Plants grow in sun or partial shade and in any free-draining soil.

Hedera hibernica (Irish ivy) is a vigorous, forgiving climber, with large lobed mid-green leaves. One plant is capable of covering a 6sq.m (20sq.ft) wall with a curtain of lush evergreen foliage. Plants are very hardy and adaptable, equally effective when grown as ground-cover.

Hedera helix 'Green Ripple' is a sumptuous ivy, 2m (6ft) high with a similar spread, and very hardy. Its gleaming evergreen leaves – jagged and lobed, with a long central point – have contrasting lighter veins, producing a rich tapestry of foliage perfect for covering tree stumps or sprawling over low walls.

Passiflora caerulea.

Parthenocissus tricuspidata 'Veitchii' is a vigorous selected form of Boston ivy producing a stunning autumn feast of colour as its three-pointed leaves turn rich reddish-purple. The display is enhanced by the matt blue berries that often linger long after the leaves have fallen. Plants grow to 20m (65ft) high with a similar spread and use tendrils to climb, so offer support with tensioned wires to help growth quickly clothe a bland wall.

Tender climbers

Mild gardens and conservatories have their share of outstanding climbers, some of which compensate for their frost-tenderness with exotically glamorous displays of colour.

Billardiera longiflora is a slender Australian climber that will just about survive outdoors in the mildest parts of Britain; elsewhere it is a superb subject for a frost-free conservatory. It is a dainty plant, with slender leaves and solitary summer flowers, greenish-yellow and bell-shaped, followed in autumn and winter by striking rich blue fruits. Plants grow best in partial shade and well-drained soil, and can reach 2m (6ft) high.

Mutisia decurrens (climbing gazania) produces brilliant vermilion, gazania-like blooms, 10cm (4in) in diameter, throughout the summer. Plants need a warm sheltered position in rich soil or a container mix of loam-based and multipurpose compost. They use tendrils to climb, so need a good support structure, and, when pampered, grow 3m (10ft) high.

Passiflora caerulea (blue passion flower) can be grown outdoors in the mildest gardens and sheltered spots, but thrives in a warm conservatory. It is renowned for its large intriguing white blooms with pink flushes and a crown of blue or purple. Growth can be rampant, with plants reaching 10m (32ft) in a sunny position and well-drained soil or compost.

Plumbago auriculata, syn. *Plumbago capensis* (Cape leadwort) produces beautiful, clear sky-blue flowers in neat clusters or trusses, almost any time from summer to winter. The fast-growing plants soon reach 5m (16ft), but need the protection of a warm conservatory or well-lit room, with temperatures 7°C (45°F) or more for stems to remain green and active.

Sollya heterophylla (bluebell creeper) has green oval-shaped leaves on slender stems, and sky-blue bells that appear in flushes between early summer and late autumn. Another climber for a sunny conservatory where temperatures remain above 7°C (45°F), it grows best in an equal mix of loam and multipurpose composts, and can reach 3m (10ft) tall.

TREES AND SHRUBS

'Planting a tree helps create a wildlife-friendly envelope in any garden.'

T O MY EYE, A GARDEN without a tree looks unfinished, and there is a tree for all but the tiniest plot. Shrubs have an equally vital role to play; whether deciduous or evergreen, large or small, they provide the backbone to the planting scheme. Both are vital for creating structure and a sense of permanence. They bring longevity to a garden the moment they are planted, and add interest to the garden throughout the seasons. Planting trees is an act of faith in the future, and with that goes a certain amount of responsibility. Because trees are the ultimate long-term plants it's essential to choose the varieties carefully, and position them with caution. Give trees and shrubs the best possible start in life, by taking time to plant them correctly and watch them closely in their early years.

A visit to any of the Royal Horticultural Society gardens reveals that their glory lies largely in the abundance of trees – some of them rare and ancient treasures – and a vast range of long-established and newly-planted shrubs. These form the bulk of the planting schemes, and are used in conjunction with other plants to form a seamless vista with year-round appeal. The men and women responsible for maintaining these woody plants have amassed many years of experience, and this know-how is an invaluable asset for the gardener who wishes to emulate the exciting effects that can be created with trees and shrubs in every garden.

LEFT: *Nyssa sylvatica* provides breathtaking autumn colour. ABOVE: *Prunus x subhirtella* 'Autumnalis'.

Trees have always been the main architects of our natural landscape. Even while the last ice age was drawing to an end, strawberry trees (*Arbutus unedo*) had settled in parts of southern Ireland, providing evergreen cover and no doubt looking terrific in the chilly autumns with their colourful clusters of white flowers and red fruits.

Other trees migrated east and north from mainland Europe, with thirty-three different species settling in Britain before the English Channel was formed and effectively halted any further movement. Those trees that made it in time then proceeded to colonize vast areas of land, and it was only when plant hunters and traders started to introduce exotic trees to the country that the landscape changed as these added variety and diversity to the rather limited stock of true native species. Both natives and later exotic arrivals can be found side by side in the RHS gardens, where you can explore a huge range of trees that enjoy growing in our hospitable climate, some of them capable of flourishing in very testing conditions.

Choosing trees

As well as being an invaluable refuge for wildlife, a tree can play a pivotal role in the design of a garden, sometimes completely altering the appearance of its surroundings. Most gardeners plant trees simply because they look great, however – deciduous trees are bold, beautiful and always changing, from the gentle unfurling of their delicate new foliage in spring until they are stark, complex silhouettes against a clear blue winter sky. Of course, many trees star at a particular season, but even if renowned for its

spring blossom or autumn leaf tints, it will still provide interest at other times of the year. Evergreen trees and shrubs retain most of their leaves throughout the year. They may lose a proportion of leaves as they naturally die, but young leaves soon cover any gaps. Deciduous trees and shrubs lose leaves in autumn and winter. Spring sees the regrowth of leaf buds and a fresh display. Some trees and shrubs are referred to as semi-evergreen. In severe weather conditions such plants may lose some or sometimes all of their leaves, but these are replaced when conditions

improve. Many plants are long-lived, surviving for decades, sometimes centuries, once established, with relatively little care and attention.

There need never be any doubt about whether to plant a tree or not, because the right kind is sure to be an asset. But trees vary in size, shape and growth rate, and also in their leaf colour and texture, so you should try to visualise how it might look when mature, to make sure you choose the most appropriate species for the site. Columnar trees, for example, fit like jigsaw pieces into gaps in borders; broad, spreading varieties can mask

eyesores beyond the boundaries; and weeping trees are good for softening boundaries and stark changes within a garden. Its eventual size will determine whether it fits neatly into your garden – most trees are little more than 3m (10ft) high when bought at garden centres and nurseries, but with the correct care will soon settle down and start expanding their branches to cover a large area, so always take note of the final height and spread as well as its preferred growing conditions before investing in any tree. (For information on planting, care of trees etc, see the Masterclass on p136.)

Eucalyptus pauciflora subsp. *niphophila* (snow gum) is one of the hardiest eucalyptus and the best kind for clay. The new evergreen leaves are orange-brown, quickly turning grey-green with red margins, while the young shoots are red, ageing to blue-white; the blue-grey and cream trunk completes this symphony of colour. Height 15m (50ft), spread 6m (20ft).

Malus hupehensis, one of many lovely crab apples, has a spring profusion of large pink buds, opening to sparkling white flowers with golden anthers followed in autumn by shiny red fruits that are irresistible to birds. Deciduous, it grows to a height and spread of 12m (40ft).

Prunus 'Kursar' produces an early spring display of bright pink flowers, just before the appearance of its reddish-bronze leaves. It is a superb deciduous small tree, growing to around 8m (26ft) high and wide.

Salix babylonica 'Tortuosa' (dragon's claw willow) bears bright green leaves in early spring that are twisted and contorted. Young twigs assume the same appearance and look terrific embellishing the upright deciduous trees, which grow fast to 12m (40ft) high and 8m (25ft) wide.

Trees for damp conditions

Some soils hold moisture for most of the year and can provide challenges for many trees. This selection adores water, whatever the time of year.

Amelanchier × *grandiflora* 'Ballerina' produces finely divided, bronze leaves in spring. Large white flowers in summer are followed by sensational autumn colour. It is a vigorous tree, growing 12m (40ft) high and 3m (10ft) wide.

Trees for clay soil

Clay soil retains moisture but in severe cases can become waterlogged. Nutrients are retained within the structure, and some trees thrive in such conditions.

Acer capillipes (red snake-bark maple) is a superb deciduous tree that can reach a height and spread of 15m (50ft). It has grey-green bark with white vertical stripes, bright red shoots that bear slender toothed leaves, glossy green for most of the season but turning glorious yellow, orange and red in autumn.

Generally speaking, a tree is a woody perennial naturally capable of growing on a single stem to a height of 6m (20ft), whereas shrubs produce several or even a thicket of shoots.

Betula nigra (river birch) grows fast to 15m (50ft) tall and 10m (33ft) wide, and has ornamental pinkish-orange bark, turning brown on older specimens and peeling in shaggy flakes. The soft-green leaves are diamond-shaped, often with silvery undersides.

Populus × jackii 'Aurora' is possibly the least aggressive poplar for gardens, and grows around 12m (40ft) high and 6m (20ft) wide. The young leaves are splashed with white, cream and sometimes pink, a startling contrast against the older dark green foliage.

Pterocarya fraxinifolia (Caucasian walnut) is a 25m (80ft) high by 20m (70ft) tall tree for large spaces. It produces suckers that need removal to prevent the tree overcrowding itself. Remove them by scraping the soil away from the base of the plant, and then pulling the suckers away from the parent as close as you can get to the main root system. Then replace the soil. In summer greenish-yellow catkins drape the canopy, while the beautiful yellow autumn leaf tints are stunning.

Sorbus aucuparia (mountain ash, rowan) supplies more red berries in a good year than most blackbirds can cope with, together with vibrant autumn red tints on the prettily divided leaves; another highlight is its grey downy buds in winter. It is 15m (50ft) tall and 5m (15ft) wide.

Trees for cold exposed positions

Cold exposed sites can be troublesome for some plants. There are trees that will happily grow in such hostile positions, and if planted in groups, can provide protection for other plants. Planted as individuals they will provide welcome structure.

Acer pseudoplatanus (sycamore) is a European native brought by the Romans to Britain, where it has thrived ever since. The large leaves create dense shade, its fissured bark hosts ferns and mosses in damp places, and its wood is revered for its hardness. Sycamores reach 25m (80ft) high and 15m (50ft) wide, and can eventually dominate woodland.

Fagus sylvatica (common beech) is a truly noble native, ultimately growing more than 30m (100ft) high and 15m (50ft) wide, but in the shorter term it is a superb choice for a hedge. Its stunningly bright young leaves gleam against the silvery-grey bark and then turn rich copper in autumn, lasting right through winter on young trees and hedges.

Laburnum × watereri 'Vossii' (Voss' laburnum) bears glossy green leaves in spring, followed by long pendulous strings of yellow flowers in early summer – these tassels may be 60cm (24in) long and produce brown seedpods in autumn. About 8m (26ft) tall by 8m (26ft).

Populus nigra (black poplar) is a large tree, growing fast to 30m (100ft) tall and 20m (70ft) wide, and looks superb in bold groups and large-scale plantings, or as a screen and windbreak. The shiny bright green leaves are diamond-shaped, while its catkins are dark red and appear in mid-spring.

Tilia cordata (small-leaved lime) has leathery heart-shaped leaves that are dark green on the upper surface, paler beneath. At 30m (100ft) tall and 15m (50ft) wide, it is another large tree and – like most native species – can withstand severe exposure. Only consider planting this where it can fully develop and not hinder other plants.

Trees with outstanding foliage

Flowers can festoon trees, but it's the colourful or eye-catching foliage that gets gardeners talking.

Acer japonicum 'Vitifolium' is a beautiful Japanese maple with broad, fan-shaped, green leaves, that colour up in autumn. Avoid cold winds and early sun to prevent leaf scorch. Grows 6m (20ft) tall and 7m (23ft) wide.

Aralia elata (Japanese angelica tree), sometimes seen as a shrub, is most impressive when grown as a 10m (30ft) by 10m (30ft) tree. Its leaves are huge, gathered in ruffs near the tips of stems, and come alight in autumn in brilliant shades of yellow, orange and purple.

Idesia polycarpa, 15m (50ft) by 12m (40ft), is a stunning tree with scarlet leaf stalks and large shiny green leaves, bronzy purple when young. In a warm season older trees produce red berries after the midsummer fragrant white blooms.

The cream and green leaves of *Aralia elata* 'Aureovariegata', seen here at RHS Garden Rosemoor, are elegantly beautiful.

Paulownia tomentosa has enormous soft triangular leaves, up to 40cm (16in) long on adult plants and born on pink leaf stalks. Large upright heads of lilac pink flowers appear before the leaves in May. It needs a warm position to grow to 15m (50ft) high and 10m (30ft) wide. Flowers can be sacrificed if you want impressive leaf size. Cut shoots hard back in spring and remove all resultant shoots bar one. The leaves on the remaining shoot will be enormous.

Trachycarpus fortunei (Chusan palm) is the hardiest palm for gardens in the United Kingdom. Its deep green, fan-shaped leaves are divided into 50–60 slender lobes, each fraying at the end. It is slow growing, eventually reaching 10m (30ft) by 2.5m (8ft), and thrives best in a sheltered position.

Trees with autumn and winter appeal

Trees add interest throughout the year, but in autumn and winter their leaves and stems can bring much appreciated colour to a garden.

Acer griseum (paperbark maple) is glorious, especially on acid soils and in full sun, when its flaking cinnamon brown bark freely peels. In autumn the foliage turns orange and red. Height 10m (30ft), spread 10m (30ft).

Cercidiphyllum japonicum (Katsura tree) is a graceful, sophisticated tree, growing fast to 20m (70ft) high and 15m (50ft) wide or more in moist soil, with heart-shaped leaves that smell of caramel once they have fallen. Before this, they turn rich shades of yellow, pink and red. A tree to lend elegance to any landscape.

Liquidambar styraciflua 'Worplesdon' (sweet gum) is a superb choice for autumn colour, rivalling the best Japanese maples. The star-shaped leaves of this outstanding variety turn fiery red, orange and yellow before falling. Specimens grow 25m (82ft) high by 12m (40ft).

Parrotia persica (Persian ironwood) is a glorious showstopper. In late summer some of the dark green leaves turn yellow, then rich orange and red in autumn, and finally deep crimson before falling. The flaking greyish bark and tiny red flowers are winter and early spring bonuses. Height and spread 10m (30ft).

Picrasma quassioides (quassia tree) is a rarely grown 10m (30ft) by 8m (25ft) tree, with a sensational autumn symphony of yellow, orange and red tints. The dark-purple shoots, scarlet buds and bright red summer fruits are additional ornamental features. Best in acid or neutral soils.

Prunus × *subhirtella* 'Autumnalis' (autumn cherry) flowers at any time between late summer through to early spring, its delicate pink and white blooms appearing on otherwise bare branches. It is eager to please and easy to grow, to 8m (26ft) high and wide.

Liquidambar styraciflua 'Worplesdon' will put on one of the best autumn leaf colour displays of any tree or shrub.

Trees with spring and summer appeal

When bulbs and herbaceous plants are at their best, there are also many trees that are glorious in spring and summer, and offer restful shade for an overworked gardener.

Cercis siliquastrum (Judas tree) is happy in warm summers and sheltered sites. Before its round grey-green leaves completely unfurl, clusters of rosy lilac pea-like flowers smother branches in April, often growing straight out of the bark. A beautiful tree, 10m (30ft) high and wide in favourable conditions.

Davidia involucrata (handkerchief tree, pocket-handkerchief tree, ghost tree, dove tree) is one of the best choices for the May garden. Its true flowers, small and purple, are held between two white bracts, one the size of a leaf, the other half that size, and both thin and papery, so they flutter in the breeze. Specimens grow 20m (65ft) tall and 10m (30ft) wide in soil that must never dry out. Ensure young trees are well watered after planting and during establishment.

Cercis siliquastrum, here trained with multiple stems, requires warm sheltered conditions but will reward you with masses of flowers.

Trees can be grown in containers, but they will need watering daily for much of the year and feeding annually. Tree roots in containers are vulnerable to frost as they lack deep soil insulation.

Embothrium coccineum (Chilean fire bush) is a spectacular small tree or large shrub, with a height of 10m (30ft) and spread 5m (15ft), for gardens in mild, wet areas. Bunches of bright orange-red flowers open in late spring and look sensational. The leathery leaves are semi-evergreen.

Gleditisia triacanthos 'Sunburst' is a golden honey locust, with bright yellow young growth in late spring that darkens to green in the height of summer. Branches are flexible and smooth, making it one of the best golden trees for windy areas. Height 25m (82ft) and spread 10m (30ft).

Liriodendron tulipifera (tulip tree) has unmistakable foliage. Its large, oddly shaped leaves, lobed with a central point, are light green at first, turning butter yellow in autumn. The green and orange tulip-shaped blooms start appearing when trees are about 20 years old. The roots are brittle, so be careful when planting. Growth can reach 30m (100ft) by 15m (50ft) in sunny positions.

Trees suitable for smaller gardens

Think of trees and many people think of vast parklands, but there are varieties that are suitable for smaller gardens. Easy to grow and delightful to look at, they add shelter and structure to a garden.

Arbutus × *andrachnoides* is a robust evergreen tree that grows slowly to 7m (22ft) by 8m (25ft). Its leaves are glossy rich green, and the white flowers appear in late autumn or spring, but the real attraction is its fascinating purplish bark that flakes in strips to leave smooth orange-brown patches.

Catalpa bignonioides 'Aurea' is a golden version of the Indian bean tree, and a good choice if you want large floppy, bright yellow leaves. Grow it in a sheltered spot shaded from scorching sun and prune it regularly for the largest, brightest leaves. The tree branches low down and shoots can grow over 60cm (2ft) a year. Unfortunately, the tips of the shoots do not ripen and are damaged by cold weather, so prune them to one bud above the main trunk to keep trees in shape and in good health. The tree will eventually reach a height and spread of 10m (30ft).

Eucryphia glutinosa (nirrhe) bears masses of large flowers in July and August, glistening white and fragrant. The toothed leaves are sometimes semi-evergreen and turn orange-red in autumn. A tree that appreciates neutral to acid soil and protection from cold winds, and grows slowly to about 10m (32ft) high and 6m (20ft) wide.

Oxydendrum arboreum (sorrel tree) needs acid soil and some winter shelter, and will grow as a large shrub up to 10m (32ft) high, or a 15m (50ft) by 8m (25ft) tree where really happy. Its deeply serrated leaves are glossy-green with greyish-green undersides. White flowers in sprays up to 25cm (10in) long appear in late summer, followed by white fruits just as the leaves turn brilliant scarlet and then deep red.

Sophora japonica 'Pendula' (weeping pagoda tree) has stiffly drooping branches clothed in long elegant leaves made up of many small leaflets. Older trees produce creamy-white fragrant pea-flowers on long clusters in late summer, followed in a good year by conspicuous seedpods. Specimens grow slowly to 8m (26ft) by 3m (10ft).

Successful tree planting

Andrew Lodge is Senior Supervisor in the Estate and Development Department of the RHS Garden at Hyde Hall, and his job is to oversee and carry out all the work needed to maintain and develop the grounds there.

Trees make the environment a better place to live in, but you do not need a forest of oaks to produce a significant difference in your surroundings. Ornamental trees in any garden supply habitats for wildlife, create shade for plants and give height to designs, often adding colour, sounds and sculptural form thoughout the year. Some gardeners are a little nervous about introducing trees and wary of their mature size or the possible effects of spreading root growth. There is no need to be worried, however, provided you choose the best kind of tree for the site, as the gardeners at the RHS gardens will confirm – they plant enough trees in the course of their work, so they should know a thing or two about them.

Andrew Lodge believes that planting trees is essential when creating a superb garden for people to visit, and also indispensable for encouraging wildlife into the area. As a result, thousands of trees are planted every year at RHS Garden Hyde Hall, some of them purely ornamental while others are intended as natural windbreaks to protect areas of the garden. Whatever your reason for planting a tree, he maintains that it will be your legacy for the future if you set about it the right way.

Sorbus aucuparia produces a fantastic show of shiny berries in autumn.

Planting a tree

1 Fork or dig a metre-square area for planting, work in plenty of organic matter such as garden compost, and dust the surface evenly with an organic fertilizer. Dig a hole 15cm (6in) larger than the tree's container, and fork over the base to improve drainage. Add organic matter to the excavated soil and mix thoroughly.

2 Stand the tree, in its container, in the centre of the hole. Lay a garden cane across the hole as a guide to check that the surface of the compost in the pot matches the surrounding soil level.

3 Remove the tree from its container and settle in position in the hole. Partly refill around the rootball with the excavated soil/compost mixture, and evenly tread it firm.

4 Add and firm more soil mix until the surface is level, and water well, ideally with saved rainwater. Mulch the whole planting site with woodchips or shredded bark to conserve moisture, but keep it 5–8cm (2–3in) away from the trunk.

Andrew's top tree selection

Oak The English or pedunculate oak, *Quercus robur*, grows fast to about 35m (115ft), especially in heavy clay soils, and is one of the best species for native wildlife. The Armenia or Pontine oak, *Quercus pontica*, is a handsome tree, only 8m (26ft) high and suitable for smaller gardens; it has bright green leaves, soft blue-grey on their underside, and mahogany-red acorns in autumn.

Ash Common ash, *Fraxinus excelsior*, tolerates poor soils and exposed conditions, and grows quickly to 25m (80ft) tall, adding bold structure to large gardens and country hedgerows. For yellow shoots and black winter buds, grow *Fraxinus excelsior* f. *diversifolia*. The golden leaves on trees 20m (65ft) tall are wonderful in spring.

Hawthorn *Crataegus monogyna*, the common hawthorn, quickthorn or may, is a familiar hedgerow feature. Growing to 10m (32ft), it has masses of white spring flowers, followed by trusses of small glossy red fruits adored by wildlife. The Oriental thorn, *C. orientalis* (syn. *C. laciniata*) (above), is a superb 6m (20ft) tree, with glossy green leaves, prolific white/pink blooms and large orange-red fruits.

Tree roots can spread as far from the trunk as the tree is high, so

be cautious if you are planning to grow trees near buildings.

Allow a safe distance of about 30m for most popular varieties.

- Keep young trees safe from rabbit and deer damage by surrounding their trunks in wire netting or spiral guards. Plastic planting tubes or shelters can protect and create a microclimate around the tree, which improves their growing conditions. Most plastic guards are slipped over the tree from above, which can force some branches to the ground unless you hold them firmly upwards. The guard should be taller than the tree's support to prevent the trunk from rubbing against the stake. Push its base into the soil to exclude voles.

- Clear all vegetation from around the base of newly planted trees, and keep this area weed-free with a mulch or planting mat for 2–3 years. This reduces competition for water and nutrients, one of the commonest causes of new trees failing to thrive.

- On heavy clay add organic matter to a large area of surrounding soil. If you confine compost to the planting hole, it could act as a sump, collecting water draining from all round and either discouraging roots from growing beyond the improved planting area or even killing them altogether from waterlogging.

- Check the condition of tree ties at least annually, and ideally every couple of months during the growing season. Adjust them if they are too loose or tight, and replace any that are worn out.

Tips from Hyde Hall

- Choose a specimen with few or no roots pushing through the base of its pot. A lot of visible roots indicates the tree is potbound and may not grow away well.
- Be discriminating: a tree with a satisfying shape and a strong undamaged leading branch will grow into something you love much more quickly than a misshapen specimen.
- Leave trees in their pots until the last minute, water them well and allow to drain just before planting, and make sure bare roots are not allowed to dry out while you prepare the planting hole.
- Prepare the site thoroughly, because planting time is the first and last chance of getting soil conditions right and the tree could be there for a very long time.
- Water newly planted trees for the first year to ensure good root growth. A weekly soaking with 18ltr (4gal) of saved rainwater is far more useful than daily dribbles, and helps encourage deep roots that will provide anchorage and find their own water.

Bare-root and container-grown trees

Bare-root trees are good value for money and are usually bought from nurseries, which can often supply a wide range of varieties, including rare kinds and extra-large specimens. November is a good month to buy and plant them, although any time up to the beginning of March is acceptable.

Container-grown trees are available from retailers and are usually limited to the most popular varieties. They tend to be more expensive than bare-root plants because a lot of time and effort has been invested in their care, but many gardeners find them more manageable, and they can be bought and planted virtually all year round.

Never plant any tree into frozen soil, though – it will be hard work for you and potentially lethal for the tree.

Staking

Some new trees need support for the first few years after planting, especially in exposed positions. The recommended type of stake has changed over the years from an upright pole as tall as the top of the clear tree trunk, to a short stake, driven in at an angle and attached low down on the trunk. This allows the tree to flex with the wind, which strengthens the base of the trunk, stimulates the growth of anchorage roots and altogether increases the chances of rapid establishment.

RHS KNOW-HOW

• Trees can be bought with their roots and surrounding soil wrapped in hessian. When planting these root-balled trees, never remove the sacking or netting because this may cause the rootball to collapse. Roots can grow easily through the hessian, which in time will degrade.

• A mulch is a valuable aid to establishment and uninterrupted growth. One of its effects is to stabilize soil conditions, so never mulch dry soil because the covering will act as a barrier and stop water percolating through.

1 After planting the tree, drive a 1m (3ft) stake into the side of the planting hole at an angle of 45°. Do not damage any tree roots.

2 The top of the stake should be about 60cm (24in) above the ground and close to – but not touching – the tree trunk.

3 Nail the buckle of an adjustable tree-tie to the stake and secure round the trunk, interposing a spacer to prevent bark abrasion against the stake. Finally tighten to allow controlled movement.

Cut out at the base any plain green shoots in a variegated shrub. These are reverting to the original species and can outgrow the variegated portion. Variegated plants in shade often develop plain branches in an attempt to catch maximum sunlight.

Shrubs

Most great gardens depend on a strong core collection of shrubs, selected and combined according to their season – or seasons – of interest to ensure a spectacular display all the year round. All four RHS gardens are packed with gorgeous shrubs, for example, demonstrating the range of choices available, with suitable species and varieties for every aspect or soil type. Bare soil is inexcusable: whether your garden shares the cold winters of RHS Garden Harlow Carr, the high rainfall at RHS Garden Rosemoor, the seasonal dryness of RHS Garden Hyde Hall or the varied and challenging conditions experienced at RHS Garden Wisley, there are shrubs that will not just survive there, but positively thrive.

Using shrubs in the garden

Shrubs are pivotal feature plants. Evergreens – shrubs that retain their leaves all year round – provide a strong backbone to a garden design, and when the lush herbaceous growth of flowering perennials has died down for winter, the evergreens stand out clear and proud, supplying interest in the bleakest of months. Deciduous shrubs have a more obvious seasonal cycle, from bud-burst to leaf-fall, but most can participate in the garden's colour and structure at any time of year, even in winter, when their bare forms are embroidered with hoar frost or a dusting of snow.

They associate readily with all plant types, both in close combination, as in predominantly herbaceous borders where they offer contrast and even support for the softer, less disciplined growth of flowering perennials, or alone as carefully positioned focal points. As your eyes feast on a perennial mixed border in full bloom, a visually strong shrub with its own distinct form and foliage acts as a highlight or punctuation mark that supplies relief from the surrounding riot of glorious colour.

Designers often use shrubs as focal points. These draw the eye down particular vistas, not to diminish the impact of intervening plants, but to supply a feeling of direction and gentle guidance – offer an invitation to explore and it will invariably be taken up. Shrubs are the light at the end of many garden tunnels. Many have other, incidental talents and may be grown as weed-suppressant ground cover, as barriers or screens to deflect wind, noise and visual intrusion, or as wall plants for training on upright surfaces, especially to complement the lower growth of true climbers.

Caring for shrubs

Most hardy shrubs are virtually self-sufficient and, once established, do not need or even appreciate mollycoddling. Very often the only intervention necessary is a certain amount of training and pruning to match the extent of growth to the available space, maintain a pleasing shape, or simply to remove any dead or diseased branches. Sharp secateurs are essential for this, and it is vital to cut just above a bud, ideally one pointing in the direction you would like future growth to take.

Planting can take place any time of the year with container-grown specimens, available in many sizes from the smallest – 9cm (3in) pots called liners – to fully mature specimens growing in massive containers. The method of planting is very much the same, irrespective of size.

Enrich the soil in the planting area with plenty of organic matter before you position the shrub. Ease the plant from the pot and place it in the hole – you should be able to fit both hands comfortably around the sides of the rootball. Then backfill the hole with the soil – ensuring the plant remains at the same depth as it was in the pot – firming as you go, and finally tread firm. Once the plant is settled in place, water it well, then mulch it generously with organic matter, keeping the mulch clear of the stems. Continue to water the plant during dry weather and take care not to skimp in the early years: empty a full watering can for each shrub.

Even though you can plant all year round, early spring or autumn are definitely the best times. In early spring the plant is just stirring and showing signs of life, and it will hardly notice being knocked from its pot and transplanted in its natural urge to grow. In autumn growth is slowing down, but the roots will remain active in the warm, moist soil even as the top growth prepares for winter. Do avoid planting in freezing weather or when the soil is waterlogged, as these are both hostile, potentially lethal conditions.

Shrubs need a good balance of nutrients to survive and thrive. Although the soil provides these, they gradually become exhausted unless you replenish them in good time. Plants have a large appetite for three major plant nutrients:

Nitrogen feeds healthy leaf growth; a plant lacking in nitrogen will have small, sickly leaves.

Phosphates are responsible for healthy roots. A deficiency causes stunted root growth and gives leaves a symptomatic purplish tinge.

Potash supports healthy flowers and fruit. A plant that lacks phosphates will have smaller, paler flowers than usual and low fruit yields.

General-purpose fertilizers contain all three nutrients. Manufacturers are legally obliged to declare the percentage of each nutrient in their product, and this is expressed as a three-figure formula in the order nitrogen, phosphates and

Take soil samples from several parts of the garden to ascertain its pH.

Acidity levels may vary considerably between different areas, offering

a selection of sites for shrubs with different soil requirements.

potash. A balanced fertilizer, ideal for shrubs, contains equal percentages of each of these three – 7:7:7, for example. Such a fertilizer is ideal for scattering on the surface of the soil and gently hoeing in before planting.

Gardeners also have a choice between organic and inorganic fertilizers. Organic fertilizers are derived from animals or vegetables and are released slowly into the soil, supplying plants with a steady diet over a long period of time. Inorganic ('chemical') fertilizers are fast-acting and give plants a quick boost, often taking effect within two days.

Planning before planting

If you can match the right plant to the site, the amount of care it will require is minimal, whereas battling against your local conditions can expose a plant to unnecessary stress. Even squeezing a shrub that wants to grow large into a small space can cause trouble – continual hard pruning not only spoils its appearance but also eventually weakens it and could invite pests and diseases to take a hold – and it might also suffer from competition for water, nutrients and light. So when purchasing or siting a shrub, check its growth rate, eventual size and cultural requirements.

The status of the soil is important. Rhododendrons need acid soil to survive, for example, and forcing them to grow in chalky soil will turn the leaves yellow and cause plants to sicken and eventually die. It is worth the small expense of testing the acidity of your soil by checking its pH, which stands for potential of hydrogen, the usual measure of soil acidity or alkalinity. A neutral soil has a reading of pH 7.0;

anything lower is acidic, while higher readings are progressively more alkaline. Home test kits are available from most garden retailers.

The soil's structure is also a vital factor. Clay soils retain more water than sandy soil, often becoming waterlogged in prolonged wet weather. Nutrients are washed out of light, sandy, and naturally well-drained soils by rain, but are held firmly around roots in clay soils. Chalky soils are something else altogether, and often feature a hard pan of chalk beneath a shallow depth of topsoil.

You have two options with your soil: either accept it and plant according to its type, or try to amend it. Digging in masses of organic matter will help both clay and sandy soils by breaking up large clay clods and bulking up porous sand. Large amounts of grit will also ease waterlogged or heavy soil. These are local or superficial improvements though, and changing the soil substantially or permanently is both unrealistic and unnecessary. Somewhere out there is a shrub suited to your soil.

Growing shrubs in containers is the answer to an incompatible soil type. You can choose the compost – which allows you to grow azaleas, rhododendrons and camellias, for example, in a garden made up of otherwise hostile alkaline soil – and you can influence the drainage of the soil, so that lavender can thrive where the garden is full of waterlogged clay soil. The other great benefit of container-growing is that you can move plants round the garden as they develop, bringing those in flower to the fore and then moving them into the background as others take over. Anything will grow in a container if you provide enough root run and remember to water and feed when required.

The amount of sunlight a plant receives can be vital. Some revel in bright light that would make shade-lovers shrivel; some variegated plants revert to plain green if they have insufficient light. Watch how sun and shade change in your garden during the day – a border slumbering in deep morning shade may well bask in sun by midday. The amount of light changes as a season progresses too, with full early spring exposure under deciduous trees allowing bulbs to grow and flower before they are eased into dappled light as the leaf canopy unfolds. Houses can cast ever-deepening shadow over their own gardens as the sun gets lower in the autumn and winter sky. Note all these rhythms and cycles, and then plant accordingly.

Shrubs for spring display

With flower buds bursting and leaves unfurling, spring is a wonderful season to be in the garden.

Chaenomeles speciosa 'Moerloosei' is one of the prettiest japonicas or flowering quinces, with dense clusters of delicate pink and white flowers on branching plants ultimately 1.8m (6ft) high by 3m (10ft) wide. Unhappy on chalk soils, it thrives in well-drained conditions in full sun, but can tolerate some shade. An excellent wall shrub if shoots are cut back by half immediately after flowering to encourage bushy growth.

Cytisus 'Boskoop Ruby', a beautiful vigorous broom with masses of deep crimson pea-like flowers in early spring, makes a rounded plant 90cm (3ft) tall and wide. It is easy to grow in any well-drained soil without additional fertilizer, but must have full sun. Prune shoots to half their length immediately after flowering.

Fothergilla gardenii (witch alder) is a small, slow-growing shrub 90cm (3ft) high and wide that needs acid soil. It grows well in semi-shade but flowers best in full sun, with a lavish display of erect bottlebrush heads of fragrant white flowers. Its crimson autumn leaf tints are memorable.

Lindera obtusiloba grows steadily to 3m (10ft) tall and wide, and enjoys semi-shade, moist acid soils and shelter from cold winds. Its aromatic foliage is bright green but turns a rich buttery yellow in autumn and makes an excellent foil for the mustard yellow flowers in spring.

Osmanthus delavayi, a rounded shrub growing slowly to 4m (13ft) all round, produces masses of scented white flowers among the glossy evergreen leaves. It needs fertile well-drained soil in sun or semi-shade. Prune back by one-third after flowering to keep plants compact.

Viburnum carlesii 'Diana' is a reliable shrub, up to 1.5m (5ft) tall and wide, with red buds that open into perfumed reddish-pink flowers that fade to white. The young foliage is often tinged with purple. Not fussy about sun or shade, or soil type, it benefits from plenty of organic matter.

Summer shrubs

Shrubs that flower in summer can offer a sensory blend of colours jostling for attention, perfumes lingering in the still warm air, and foliage that invites the touch.

Abelia 'Edward Goucher' is a stunning shrub, semi-evergreen in milder areas and rarely more than 1.5m (5ft) tall and wide, and therefore suitable for smaller gardens. The young leaves are prettily bronzed, and are followed by a display of soft pink and white flowers that lasts from early summer often into winter. It grows steadily in well-drained soil and full sun.

Buddleja crispa has densely woolly stems and deliciously scented lilac flowers with orange throats in late summer. In full sun and well-drained soil, it grows fast to 3m (10ft) high by 1.8m (6ft) wide, even larger if planted and trained against a warm wall.

Callistemon sieberi (alpine bottlebrush) is the hardiest species, growing slowly in well-drained soil and full sun to 1.5m (5ft) high and 90cm (3ft) wide. Its dense foliage of slim evergreen leaves is a perfect foil for the clusters of soft lemon-yellow flowers in late summer. In really cold areas, grow in a container and overwinter in a cold greenhouse.

Ceanothus 'Blue Mound' is the pick of the Californian lilacs, with dense clusters of deep blue flowers smothering the evergreen framework of glossy leaves. It can grow 1.8m (6ft) each way, and prefers well-drained soil in full sun. Trim the sideshoots after flowering to encourage bushiness and prevent bare lower stems.

Hibiscus syriacus 'Ardens' is a compact plant, slow-growing to 3m (10ft) by 1.8m (6ft), with rosy-purple blooms, each with a maroon blotch at its base. Grow in well-drained soil and full sunlight. The new deep green foliage appears later than on most other shrubs in the garden.

Itea ilicifolia has glossy evergreen leaves and attractive fragrant flowers, greenish-white and rather like catkins, in early summer. It grows slowly to 3m (10ft) each way in semi-shade. Avoid soils that dry out in summer, and add plenty of organic matter at planting time.

The foliage of *Ceanothus* 'Blue Mound' is completely covered in clusters of flowers late in spring and in early summer.

Autumn colour

Shrubs are indispensable for an autumn display of leaf colours and flowers, just as the season is drawing to a close.

Acer palmatum 'Sango-kaku' (formerly 'Senkaki') has coral-red branches and leaves that turn the softest of yellows in autumn. It grows slowly to 6m (20ft) high and 5m (16ft) wide. It is content in sun or semi-shade, and in any soil that is not waterlogged.

Ceratostigma willmottianum (Chinese plumbago) produces vivid rich blue flowers from late summer to late autumn, when its oval green leaves turn various shades of red. In full sun and any well-drained soil it grows steadily to 90cm (3ft) high and wide. Cut out dead growth in spring to avoid disease problems.

Clerodendrum bungei (glory flower) produces fragrant clusters of deep pink or reddish purple flowers on an upright, slow-growing bush eventually 2.4m (8ft) each way. Thriving in sun or semi-shade, it needs well-drained soil and benefits from a winter mulch of fallen leaves to protect roots from harsh weather.

Euonymus alatus (winged spindle) is a most reliable source of autumn colour, its foliage turning a breathtaking brilliant crimson as temperatures start to fall. Slowly growing to 1.5m (5ft) high and 2.4m (8ft) wide, it is not fussy about the soil, and thrives in sun or semi-shade, although it should be watered well in summer if planted in full sun. It also performs well in large containers, the root restriction produces even better autumn colour than border-grown specimens.

Euonymus alatus var. *apterus* never fails to impress autumn visitors to the RHS gardens.

Hamamelis × *intermedia* 'Jelena' is a gorgeous witch hazel, with large flowers of rich coppery-red that appear orange in the weak late autumn sunshine, and a sweet, heady perfume. Like many other acid-loving plants, its autumn leaf colours are fantastic shades of orange, red and copper, lighting up any sunny or semi-shaded border. It needs good drainage, and grows slowly to 5m (16ft) tall by 4m (13ft) wide.

Vaccinium arctostaphylos (Caucasian whortleberry) is another vividly colourful shrub for well-drained acid soils. Its pinkish white summer flowers are charming, while the autumn leaf tints are sensational shades of red and purple, lingering well into winter. Plants prefer light soils in sun or semi-shade, growing slowly to 3m (10ft) by 1.8m (6ft), and may be raised from seeds cleaned from the purplish-black autumn fruits.

Winter shrubs

In winter shrubs can provide valuable structure, together with unexpected colour and perfume when all else is bare and dormant.

Azara petiolaris is an elegant evergreen that grows slowly to 5m (16ft) high and wide, and produces sweetly perfumed yellow flowers in late winter. Grow it in well-drained soil, in sun or shade but ideally near the shelter of a south or west-facing wall in cold areas. As insurance, take some cuttings in late summer and overwinter them in a cold frame.

Corylus avellana 'Contorta' (corkscrew hazel) has extraordinary sculptural twisted stems, and clusters of long yellow catkins at the end of winter. Its female flowers are like tiny red sea anemones. It grows slowly to 6m (20ft) tall and 5m (16ft) wide, and likes a sunny or semi-shaded spot on well-drained fertile soil.

Daphne bholua 'Jacqueline Postill' is an upright evergreen shrub with showy, very fragrant purplish-pink and white flowers in late winter. Slow growing and ultimately 1.8m (6ft) each way, it prefers an undisturbed position in full sun, in any fertile well-drained soil that does not dry out in summer.

Jasminum nudiflorum (winter jasmine) produces bright yellow, fragrant flowers studded along bare green branches. It soon reaches 4m (13ft) high and wide in any well-drained, fertile soil. Trim after flowering to reduce the long shoots to a controllable size. This is a sprawling shrub and so may need some support for best effect.

Stachyurus praecox has buds that form in late summer and open in late winter to display delicate, pale lemon bells on long pendulous clusters. The arching reddish purple shoots spread into a shapely bush 1.8m (6ft) high and wide. Plant in sun or semi-shade, in slightly acidic well-drained soil.

Shrubs for year-round interest

Whereas some shrubs give a very seasonal, even brief performance, others work hard the whole year to earn their place in the garden.

Euonymus fortunei 'Silver Queen' is evergreen, with dark leaves margined with creamy white, later turning pink; and small white flowers in spring. It has an average growth rate, to about 3m (10ft) high by 1.8m (6ft) wide. Plant in sun or semi-shade, in fertile well-drained soil. Never let plants in full sun dry out completely.

Nandina domestica (heavenly bamboo) has
narrow evergreen leaves attractively tinged red
and pink in spring and autumn. White star-
shaped flowers appear above the stems in
summer, followed in a warm season by long-
lasting red fruits. Plant in a sunny spot in
fertile, well-drained soil, where it will steadily
grow to 1.8m (6ft) all round.

Pittosporum tenuifolium is a charming New
Zealand species, plant in a sunny sheltered
position even in mild gardens, as it is not
completely hardy, although it is best planted
against a south or west-facing wall in colder
areas. It has evergreen leaves, glossy and wavy-
edged, with purple shoots and honey-scented
purple flowers in spring. Plants need a well-
drained soil, where they can eventually reach
6m (20ft) high and 4m (13ft) wide.

Shrubs as hedges

A hedge is a line of shrubs planted closely together
so that their outlines merge seamlessly with each
other. Hedges can be tightly clipped formal features
of dense species such as yew or privet, or an
informal tapestry of flowering shrubs. Both types
have important roles, especially for marking out
boundaries, where they are hospitable to wildlife.

An informal flowering hedge is a colourful asset
and one of the easiest kinds to grow, using free-
flowering species such as wild roses, pyracantha
and spiraea; knit wild honeysuckle through the
shrubs for extra carefree colour and fragrance.
Wild creatures adore flowering hedges, using them
as food sources, refuges and breeding sites.

Informal hedges require little or no maintenance
beyond an annual trim. Formal hedges need more
regular clipping, depending on the kind of plant
used. Privet, for example, grows fast and might
require trimming every few weeks in summer to
keep it looking tidy, whereas beech hedging is
clipped to shape twice, in spring and late summer.

In the right kind of site, Leyland cypress (×
Cupressocyparis leylandii) is a valuable hedging
conifer, but it needs cutting two or three times a
year to keep it under control and robs the
surrounding soil of nutrients; it quickly outgrows
a typical back garden and really needs the large
space that RHS gardens can provide. For a
smaller, more manageable conifer, try *Thuja
occidentalis* 'Rheingold', which requires less
trimming and knits together into a dense and
attractive 4m (13ft) hedge of golden foliage that
turns rich bronze in winter. For a bright green
hedge, choose *T. occidentalis* 'Smaragd', 2.4m
(8ft) tall, and for dark green try *T. occidentalis*
'Holmstrup', up to 4m (13ft) high.

Small shrubs are used to create low hedges,
which make excellent edgings for paths and beds.
Dwarf hedging box (*Buxus sempervirens*
'Suffruticosa') is popular for heights up to 60cm
(24in), but needs clipping two, possibly three,
times a year to maintain tight walls of green
foliage. Lavender is a superb hedging plant for
herb gardens. If allowed to grow without check,
lavender can mature as a tall plant with its flowers
confined to the top of bare woody stems, whereas
regular pruning will keep the stems fully clothed
in fragrant leaves, with flowers emerging from all
round on bushy shoots. Prune all growth by half
in spring to stimulate plenty of bushy sideshoots
and a further light pruning in around late August
to remove the faded flower heads, if you wish.

PESTS AND DISEASES

Well-grown plants survive attacks from pests and diseases. Natural vigour is the best pesticide of all.

A GARDEN IS NOT A sterile place. From a wildlife perspective that is a good thing, but it does mean that plants could succumb to an attack by some pest or disease or compete for space with weeds. Do not let this discourage you – with so many potential threats around your chances of success are not slim. Many disorders are rare, cosmetic rather than disabling, or very specific, only attacking a few less common plants. You are more likely to encounter problems belonging to a small group of widespread pests or diseases. Of course, it is disheartening to see a prize specimen keel over in its prime, but there are ways to solve most of these problems.

It is easy to jump to the wrong conclusions about a mysterious symptom and assume the worst, when the problem might be cultural – perhaps a lack of a nutrient in the soil or the wrong watering regime. Many apparent diseases are in fact cultural disorders that can be reversed, and not everything that crawls or flies round the garden is a potential enemy. Weeds are defined as plants that are either uninvited or making themselves too comfortable in the garden, at the expense of the plants you did plan for, but you might be able to live with a small number of them. Always look for the simple answers before reacting, and try to avoid trouble initially by taking sensible precautions. The RHS Gardens are justifiably proud of their relative freedom from pests, diseases and weeds, but this happy state of affairs has been achieved by a little effort, a lot of planning and, above all, good gardening practices.

LEFT: RHS Garden Rosemoor is bursting with natural vigour and healthy plants as a result of regular care and good gardening practices. ABOVE: Molehills can spoil the look of any lawn.

Some pests and diseases are not specific to one plant or even one group of plants – they are not so choosy about their victims. Many of the most common pests and diseases are explored in more detail in this chapter and in relation to the situations they most often occur in, but here's a glimpse at the rogues gallery.

Pests

Aphids and caterpillars (see p154) are probably the most easily recognized pests which can, and will, at some time attack most plants. Leaf miners can burrow into the leaves of many different types of plants, causing the unmistakable tunnelling and disfigurement, while flea beetles are a problem on many vegetables of the cabbage family as well as related ornamental perennials (see p155). Vine weevils are a potential problem of any plants growing in containers and you may be unfortunate enough to experience Red spider mites in a hot summer (see p162), they are particularly prevalent in glasshouses on many different plants; outdoors they can also be a killer for many conifers. In all these cases, the secret is to catch the attacks early so as to reduce the damage.

Slugs and snails are the bain of many gardener's lives and are indiscriminate in what they will eat – seedlings, vegetables, herbs, ornamentals all look delicious to these creatures. Frustratingly, as yet no perfect solution has been found as how to control them in the garden. Chemical control is frowned upon nowadays and encouraging wildlife and other more environmentally friendly tactics are being pursued (see masterclass on p164 for more information).

Diseases

Diseases are caused by fungi, bacteria and viruses. Insects, however, may play a part in passing on diseases, particularly virus diseases. Fungi and bacteria can kill plants and are easier to diagnose than viruses, which cause stunting, malformed growth and drastically reduced cropping.

Like pests, diseases are no respecters of age and maturity, damping off is a disease which is caused by a number of different fungi, and can affect all seedlings. In the right conditions, grey mould (botrytis) will attack all soft tissue of any plant, while canker, dieback and silver leaf are a problem for both fruiting and ornamental trees.

Details on pests and diseases, especially the universal ones can appear daunting; but plants when grown well will resist many attacks and outgrow small amounts of damage. Never be put off growing a plant, or group of plants because the list of nasties waiting to pounce is long, just keep a watchful eye on your charges and nip trouble in the bud before it gets out of control.

What are weeds?

It is well documented that a weed is only a plant growing in the wrong place at the wrong time, in situations where they compete for light, water and nutrients. So getting rid of this competition with your chosen plants, especially among food crops, is essential for the intended plants to flourish. It is always best to use cultural methods of removal, rather than chemical – this means ensuring that you prepare the soil properly before planting, completely removing all traces of weeds. Any weeds that then appear after planting must be

LEFT TO RIGHT: Caterpillars munching on a rose leaf, Canker and a dandelion seedhead (*Taraxacum officinale*).

cleared as soon as possible – certainly before they have a chance to set seed.

Catching them before they seed prevents future weed generations from starting out, and is particularly important for annual weeds. These weeds, as their name suggests, only live for one growing season, but they will continue to return in future years if they get the chance to sow their abundant seeds. Annual weeds can be successfully removed by hoeing, digging and pulling out by hand before they are allowed to set seed, and hoeing small weeds to the soil surface on a sunny day means they will quickly wilt and die. Perennial weeds, however, stick around for quite a lot longer and need more brutal treatment to remove them.

Perennial weeds

These weeds – which include dandelions, horsetail, ivy or ground elder – are much tougher plants and can resist digging, hoeing and hand weeding. In fact, the more you cut and slice through the roots of these weeds the more problems you are likely to encounter as new plants will grow from each root section. You can weaken their vigour by repeatedly removing top growth and the root system, but you must make sure every last bit of root is dug out. It's best to leave the ground fallow where bad infestations of these weeds occur as they will become even harder to eradicate when concealed by ornamental plants and your desirable plants will eventually come off second best to these bullies. Specific areas of soil, especially in vegetable plots, can be covered with thick black polythene or with an old piece of carpet, as this will starve the plants of essential light and will weaken root systems. However, this method could take up to a year to work effectively and so may not be an appropriate method for less patient gardeners.

If all cultural methods of eradication fail, then there is one chemical treatment that can safely be used. Translocated weed killers based on glyphosate act by entering the plant and travelling deep into the root system. This way, glyphosate kills the entire plant – and any green plant it comes into contact with – but is deactivated when it touches the soil. Several applications will be needed to kill persistent weeds such as bindweed and ground elder. As glyphosate kills all green plant material it is therefore difficult to apply as a spray where desirable plants are growing, but it is also available in a gel formulation where application is by a small paintbrush. Coat the weed leaves with a

The familiar stinging nettle.

layer of the chemical and it is translocated down to the roots and gets into action.

In the current climate of environmental concern, less people are using chemical controls on weeds and are preferring to try cultural methods instead. Always investigate these cultural methods of eradication – hoeing, hand weeding, digging, and smothering – before resorting to chemicals. Of course, if you do decide to use chemicals, care must be taken when applying them – never spray them on a windy day and never near ponds or streams or you risk passing the chemicals on and harming other plants and creatures. Whether you use chemicals or not, don't throw weeds onto your compost heap without removing perennial roots and any flowering/seeding portions, or you will be creating more work for yourself by adding weed seeds to your garden every time you dig in compost. Once the weeds have been eradicated from an area, it can be planted up.

Susceptible situations

As mentioned before, not all diseases and pests are exclusive to one plant, and many attack a variety of plants, but some species are more susceptible to particular troubles than others. Here we will try to link the pests, diseases and weeds to some of the most relevant situations covered in this book.

Some problems can be avoided or their effects contained before they get established, so you should keep a close eye on your plants and look out for any early signs of trouble. Always remember to see problems in the context of your garden as a complete and sensitive ecosystem. Try to avoid trouble by using good gardening practices and suitable precautions or deterrents, and when problems do occur, try cultural and biological approaches – such as inviting in hard-working insect allies to help you out – before you reach for the chemicals.

Roses

Some rose varieties are more susceptible to problems than others. Choose your plants carefully and if a particular disease such as black spot or mildew is known to be prevalent in your area, select a variety that has a resistance (check with the nursery or an up-to-date catalogue). Spraying with a fungicide or insecticide is always an option, unless you are disinclined to use them, but sound cultural practices can reduce the threat before your plants begin to suffer.

Blackspot is the bête noire of roses, and is first seen on leaves as small dark spots surrounded by yellow patches, which grow larger and eventually

Ants running up and down plant shoots is often an indication of aphids. The ants do little damage themselves, but they farm aphids for honeydew and move them around plants while providing the aphids with protection from predators.

cause leaves to fall prematurely. This fungal disease spreads by means of spores, which overwinter on fallen rose leaves and can reinfect new spring growth if left on the ground, so tidy up and burn all the leaves around the base of your roses in the autumn. Prune out any stems that show signs of overwintering spores – small purple pinpricks on otherwise green or brown stems are telltale signs. There are fungicidal sprays available and spraying should start before the first symptoms are seen. It is good policy to alternate between different fungicides, to avoid resistance. Once leaves are infected the disease is difficult to shift. (See the roses on p20 for varieties that are resistant to blackspot.) Take care when watering, too, do not water the plant from above as this will encourage any spores on higher infected leaves to splash down onto uninfected ones below.

LEFT TO RIGHT: Disease shown on rose leaves: black spot, rust and powdery mildew.

Rust diseases revel in warm moist conditions, so roses are most likely to be attacked towards the end of the summer. The disease manifests itself with bright orange pustules that appear on the undersides of the leaves, and then turn black in early autumn. Culturally, it is best to remove all infected leaves as soon as you spot them, which will prevent the rust from spreading. Once you have removed them, you should burn infected leaves rather than add them to the compost heap, as the temperature there may not be high enough to kill them. Clear up any fallen leaves in autumn because, like blackspot, rust spores will overwinter on them.

The spores need a film of water on the leaf to trigger germination, so only apply water to the soil around your roses and not onto the foliage. There are fungicidal sprays available, which must be used at regular intervals according to the manufacturer's instructions. Other rust victims include leeks, mints, raspberries, plums, irises and hollyhocks.

Biological controls are the natural way to combat some common pests, especially under glass. All biological controls are available from mail order companies or from some garden retailers.

Powdery mildew is a familiar problem which is common on many outdoor and greenhouse plants, and particularly on roses. It produces white dusty deposits that disfigure the upper surfaces of leaves, especially if the weather has been dry and plants are under stress from lack of water. Make sure there is plenty of organic matter in the soil, and apply a thick mulch of compost on damp soil before the problem has a chance to develop. Still, stagnant air favours mildew, but you can increase air movement around your plants by pruning out criss-crossing branches, weak growth and surplus stems, especially if they show signs of infection – powdery mildew can attack stems, buds and flowers, as well as foliage. Pick off and burn badly infected leaves, and tidy up and burn all fallen leaves to prevent the spores from overwintering. Sprays are available, but make sure you read the instructions and precautions on the packaging (mildew sprays are not suitable for all flowers).

Caterpillars of various kinds can nibble irregular holes in the leaves of many plants, but, again, they have a penchant for roses. The best way to avoid damage is to keep a close watch on plants, especially if you notice odd holes appearing. When you find a caterpillar, pick it off and then take a wider look round, because you can assume it will not be alone. Many feed at night while predators are elsewhere, and an evening's stroll with gloves and a plastic bag can be productive. Several common birds feed on them, and you can encourage these by setting up a few leaves, laden with your picked caterpillars, on a feeding table – they may then explore further afield and help keep numbers down. Sprays such as bifenthrin,

pyrethium and rotenone are available and may be needed if plants are badly infested. As with all pests, vigilance is required, and perhaps a little tolerance: caterpillars develop into moths, and on reflection therefore you might be prepared to accept small amounts of damage.

Perennials and grasses

Shoots of perennials and grasses are irresistible to some pests and diseases. They often select the youngest, most succulent growth for attack, which can be debilitating for the plant. Gardeners should therefore monitor their plants and their state of growth, and be aware of what to look for. Act quickly to avoid longer-term problems.

Aphids may attack the soft new growth of most plants, herbaceous and woody. They assume a range of disguises – many are green, others black or yellow – and cause damage by sucking sap from the stems, leaves and flowers whilst spreading viruses between plants. They also exude a sticky substance called honeydew, on which black sooty moulds can grow, making it difficult for plant leaves to function fully. Always check the undersides of leaves for aphids, because they prefer to remain hidden and can cause real damage out of sight; distorted leaves, stems and flowers are often the signs of an aphid infestation. Their numbers increase rapidly as young aphids are born with more developing inside them. Small colonies can be squashed before they cause too much damage, but you need to patrol the garden every day. Natural predators such as ladybirds, lacewings and hoverflies can reduce aphid numbers dramatically. Ladybird larvae can be bought or collected from elsewhere in the

garden, and sprinkled onto infested plants. They eat away and mature into adult ladybirds that often stay around and breed. Sprays, such as bifenthrin and imidachloprid are available and natural products such as pyrethrum, rotenove, fatty acids or vegetable oils control aphids effectively, but they may also kill other insects, some beneficial.

Leaf miners tunnel into leaves of many shrubs and herbaceous plants, causing cream- or brown-coloured 'mines' on upper surfaces. The damage is more cosmetic than constitutional, and the only treatment is to crush them at the ends of their tunnels, or pick off and burn the infested leaves.

Flea beetles eat the upper surfaces of leaves, especially of brassicas and related plants. They cause tiny holes or cream-coloured patches where they have not completely eaten their way through. The beetles are about 3mm (⅛in) long, and may be shiny black or metallic blue, with or without yellow stripes, according to the species. They jump when disturbed, so killing them is difficult. The best policy is to grow strong plants that can soon outgrow the damage they cause. Seedlings are particularly vulnerable to attack, but can be

protected from serious injury if you use a rotenone or bifenthrin spray at the first sign of trouble. Read the label first, to make sure the chemical is suitable for the particular plants. Keep seedlings watered to ensure their rapid growth through the vulnerable phase.

Damping off is a fungal disease to which young seedlings are most prone. The seedlings start to grow normally, but after a couple of weeks they keel over and die. Close inspection reveals their stems are shrivelled and blackened, the result of infection by a combination of soil- and water-borne fungi. These are most active when the compost is wet and temperatures too high, and affects overcrowded seedlings more easily than thinly-sown ones. Never use rainwater collected and stored in a water butt to water seeds and seedlings, because fungal spores may be present. They can also survive on the remains of compost in trays and pots, so it is vital to clean thoroughly all seed containers, any capillary mats and to use only new, sterile compost. Seedlings can be watered with a protectant fungicide if you wish, such as Cheshunt compound.

Wilt is a distressing condition to witness. One day a plant is healthy, the next it has collapsed. Aster, dianthus, chrysanthemums, poppies and many other plants are susceptible to the soil-borne fungi that produce fusarium and verticillium wilts. Both of these cause leaves and stems to droop until affected plants die. Cutting open a diseased stem reveals distinctive brown staining. There is no cure, so plants must be removed and burnt – do not discard them on a compost heap because the spores will remain active and multiply when compost is spread on the soil. Avoid growing the same type of plant on the affected site.

Lawns

A well-tended lawn is rarely affected by pests, diseases or weeds because it is constantly receiving some kind of attention, and nothing has a chance to establish. The same cannot be said for rougher or poor quality lawns, which are often infiltrated by weeds that are difficult to remove. Some diseases and pests can also become troublesome, although regular mowing and maintenance can ameliorate most lawn problems.

Fairy rings are fungi that grow on your lawn in a roughly circular colony of toadstools. This expands outwards very slowly – established rings can be decades, even centuries old – and many people find them unobjectionable. They can take one of three forms, and only one really requires drastic remedial action. The first type of fairy ring is the most sinister and produces two dark bands on the lawn with a dead strip of grass in between – the rings travel outwards throughout the growing season, killing more grass as they go. Toadstools usually appear on the outer edge of the ring. The only certain treatment is to remove a ring of affected turf and soil, 45cm (18in) deep and 45cm (18in) beyond the inner and outer edges, and replace this with topsoil from elsewhere; then seed or turf the repaired area. The second type produces a dark green band of grass on the outer edge of the ring, and all you need do with this is keep the rest of the lawn as green as the outer edge by using appropriate fertilizers. The third kind is a ring of toadstools with no discoloration of the grass. Simply pick and destroy the toadstools, and avoid sweeping the lawn as this can spread the spores.

Moss is a lovely little plant – springy to walk on – but is widely cursed by gardeners throughout Britain. When it appears in a lawn, it is a symptom of wet, poorly-drained, sickly conditions underground. Waterlogged grass will be colonized by moss, as will lawns in heavy shade or on compacted soil. Sort out the shade, compaction and drainage inadequacies, and the moss will disappear. Some mosses, especially upright kinds, happily grow on dry, acid soils where grass struggles to get a roothold, but these can be prevented by correctly preparing the site before seeding or turfing. A lawn that is consistently scalped will suffer from moss that is quick to take over where the strength and vigour of the grass is reduced. There are treatments that will get rid of moss, but it always reappears if you do not tackle the underlying problems. Moss killers act within days, but usually leave bare patches that need prompt seeding or returfing to prevent weed invasions.

Clover is a nuisance in good lawns. In dry conditions, as the grass turns yellow and grows more slowly, the clover remains green and

continues to grow, creating a patchwork of colours that is unacceptable to owners of respectable lawns. The plant is easily recognised, and has pompon flowers standing upright above creeping stems that bear the distinctive three leaflets. It thrives on poor, dry soil, so cultural treatment involves using fertilizers and topdressing to improve grass growth. Before mowing, it is a good idea to rake the lawn to lift up the low clover stems and expose them to the blades of the mower. An application of 'feed and weed' fertilizer will eradicate clover without affecting the fine grasses, while the nutrients will help to green up the turf. Lawn sand is less effective and potentially damaging because over-application will damage the lawn. It is usually best to try cultural techniques before resorting to chemicals.

Buttercups are tolerated, even encouraged by many, while others abhor the presence of this rather aggressive weed. Creeping buttercups are easily controlled if they are tackled at an early stage. One or two plants can be dug up with a pointed trowel, taking care to remove all their

Fairy rings take different forms and all require different treatments.

roots. If left uncontrolled, they will colonize large areas, spreading by means of their creeping stems, which root and create new plants at frequent intervals. The roots are strong and tenacious, unaffected by a casual scuff with the foot as you stroll by – even mowing only removes a few leaves, and it is impossible to cultivate the weed away. Improving the drainage on wet soils can reduce the problem, while selective weedkillers will completely kill the weed. These chemicals act only on broad-leaved weeds, leaving the grass untouched.

Moles in – or rather under – a lawn are a contentious problem. On the one hand, many gardeners refuse to destroy these mammals; on the other, it is hard to sit back and watch the lawn being ruined by their activities. Molehills appear overnight where they have dumped excavated soil, and their tunnels often collapse, causing ruts on otherwise level turf. Since mole smokes are now illegal, if you want to destroy the creatures you can either call in a professional, who will poison them, or set a trap yourself, which is difficult to do properly and may cause unnecessary suffering. The alternative method is to drive them away, using one or more of the available deterrents. These range from simple windmills to position in the top of molehills, to battery or solar-powered devices that produce sonic pulses intended to annoy the mole into leaving. Bottles, buried in the soil with their necks protruding into the wind, are said to produce enough sound and vibration to drive moles away. All have only limited success and you may need to combine several methods. The only consolation is that the presence of a mole is usually an indication that the soil is rich and full of earthworms.

Edibles

Vegetable plants and fruit have a reputation for attracting more than their fair share of trouble, but growing your own food need not be a constant battle. Sound cultural practices and the use of resistant varieties will reduce problems to acceptable levels, while understanding the conditions that pests and diseases need in order to thrive and multiply – a large concentration of a single vulnerable crop, for example, or plants under stress from a shortage of water or nutrients – can help prevent or delay an attack.

Potato blight can be devastating to potatoes and their close relation, tomatoes. The disease manifests itself on the leaves as discoloured patches that develop white fluffy areas, and it will often go on to affect the tubers and fruits. It thrives in warm humid conditions, usually appearing around midsummer, and is impossible to suppress if weather conditions favour its spread. As soon as you see the disease on potato leaves, remove and burn the haulms, and lift the crop straightaway. If you have spotted the disease early, the tubers will be unaffected, but keep an eye on them in store, just in case any diseased spores have been washed into the soil. Affected tomato plants decline in vigour, and their fruits may also be affected; lift and burn plants at the first sign of the disease. Do not grow potatoes in soil affected by blight for at least three years – crop rotation will reduce the incidence of follow-on infection – and always keep potato and tomato plants well apart. To prevent infection, use a copper or macozeb fungicidal spray when weather conditions favour the disease.

Whiteflies on brassicas are a nuisance. They rise up in clouds as you brush past, swarming from the undersides of leaves, where they feed on the sap. Black moulds may also grow on whitefly exudates. An infestation needs to be really heavy to have a marked effect on crops, so tolerance is an acceptable response. Serious attacks can be treated with insecticidal sprays based on fatty acids or vegetable oils, which is very effective at removing adult whiteflies. Further applications will be necessary as juvenile stages mature. Tomatoes, cucumbers and other plants growing under the protection of glass or plastic are attacked by glasshouse whitefly. Biological control with the parasitic wasp *Encarsia formosa* is an effective alternative to insecticides in such situations.

Black bean aphids are fairly common from late May to August, and once installed can smother the tender growing shoots of broad beans within days;

if left untreated, the plants become stunted with deformed flowers and pods. Culturally, it is best to avoid them altogether by sowing broad beans early under cloches and pinching out the shoot tips once they have produced five trusses of flowers – if free from aphids, you will find them a tasty vegetable after gentle steaming. Five trusses will provide a good crop, and the black bean aphids have to look elsewhere for their food. Control is also possible using sprays based on bifenthrin, pyrethrum, fatty acids or vegetable oils.

Carrot fly affects carrots, parsnips, parsley and even celery. Female flies lay eggs at the base of the leaves, and hatched larvae then tunnel into the roots, which often exposes them to secondary rot, rendering the crop useless. These pests are low-flying insects and will not go over obstacles more than 60cm (24in) high, so erecting a protective barrier of fine mesh around carrot beds will keep them clean. Growing crops beneath a tunnel of horticultural fleece acts in the same way. There are some partially resistant varieties of carrot, with roots that are less palatable to the larvae; although some damage occurs, the crop as a whole is usable.

Big bud mite affects blackcurrants; tiny mites feed inside developing buds, causing them to become abnormally swollen and round (healthy buds are slim and pointed). Infested buds dry up and produce no growth in spring. Attacks first start in late spring, when the mites are blown around in the air or carried from plant to plant by insects. Inspect buds in winter, nipping out any that are swollen or rounded and burning them, then check again several times during the year. If occupied buds are left on the bushes, the mites will spread, first to other buds and then adjacent bushes. Your only option with a badly infested plant is to dig it up and burn it.

Grey mould can attack any part of any plant. Its spores are naturally everywhere, waiting for the moist stagnant conditions they need to start growing. They usually enter a plant through a cut or wound, where they cause the soft tissues to rot as the fungus develops out of sight – the first inkling you have of its presence may be a fuzzy greyish-white surface growth that appears as more

spores are produced. Fungicidal sprays are no longer available, and it is better to stop the fungus taking hold in the first place by practising good hygiene in the garden. Ensure air circulation is good in the greenhouse, and around plants. Clean up any debris that could harbour spores and remove all dead or dying flowers and leaves. On woody plants, cut out infected areas to well beyond the site of infection.

Water

Crystal clear water is a joy in many artificial water features, whereas a teeming population of visible wildlife is the whole point of some ponds. A problem arises when a pond fails to recover from the distinctly murky soup that is seen soon after planting up, an indication that the natural chemical composition of the pond water is out of balance.

Green water in ponds and pools can choke wildlife as well as look unappealing. It is a symptom of imbalance, possibly caused by

nutrients running into the water from the surrounding garden. Shade is an important control because it restricts algae to tolerable populations, and the best way to supply this shade is by introducing and maintaining enough surface floating plants. Remove dead leaves and wildlife from ponds because their decay releases nutrients into the water. Treating the problem with chemicals or by suspending barley straw or pads of lavender stems in the water will clear ponds in the short-term, but the only durable answer is to redress the imbalance. If all else fails, it may be necessary to install a filter to keep the water clean, particularly in small ponds where the results of any imbalance are often magnified out of proportion.

Water plants have relatively few damaging pests, which is fortunate as all pesticides are dangerous to fish and other pondlife. If aphids occur on water lilies in small ponds it is feasible to wipe them off the foliage by hand. One significant disease is water-lily crown rot, which can devastate a collection of water lilies. The first signs of trouble are yellowing leaves, followed by blackened areas where the leaves join the crown. Eventually the foliage floats off and rots in the water. Removing infected plants from the water is the only way to control the disease, and if this is widespread you might need to dispose of all the plants, and then drain and clean the pond. When introducing new water lilies, always check them carefully and reject any with soft black areas on their crowns.

Herons are majestic birds, but they can eventually empty a pond of its fish collection. A patient and persistent wading bird, a heron hunts by day and will stand motionless in a pond waiting for an unsuspecting fish to swim past, when it will suddenly lunge with a lethal stab of its bill. Physical barriers are the only effective way to avert a heron attack, preventing the bird from wading into the pond in the first place. Canes inserted into the ground around a pond and linked with string will deter most herons. Model herons have been known to scare them off, and sonic devices triggered by the approach of a heron are also successful.

Climbers

Climbers are generally self-sufficient and prone to few ailments, their vigour helping them to outgrow infections without your even noticing. Occasionally a pest or disease could gain the upper hand and needs to be controlled. As with all plants, robust well-grown specimens are not as susceptible to attacks as plants in poor health.

Clematis wilt looks alarming, especially when a previously healthy plant collapses literally overnight, its topgrowth often dying within a fortnight. If you check first and find that the plant is not short of water and that its stem has not been damaged by over-enthusiastic hoeing, you can conclude that clematis wilt is to blame. This is a fungal disease that usually enters the plant through the leaves, then spreads rapidly down the stems. Only the topgrowth is affected, and plants can grow out of the disease, their unharmed buried buds growing up through the soil surface to produce new stems. Planting new clematis deeper than they were growing in their pots encourages plenty of underground buds to form as an insurance. There is no spray effective against clematis wilt, and your only option is to cut off the dead growth at surface level – do not compost it – and wait for the plant to revive from below ground.

Downy mildew indicates its presence with patches of fluffy white mould, purple-tinged at the edges and growing on the undersides of leaves. Vines and Virginia creeper can suffer occasionally. Downy mildew enjoys damp conditions and stagnant air, so a sound precaution is to improve air circulation by pruning out any branches that cross each other in the centre of susceptible plants; remove and burn any leaves that show signs of the disease. There are no chemicals available to control downy mildew, and do not attempt to use any fungicides that are designed for powdery mildew – although they sound similar, the two fungi are completely different and should be treated differently.

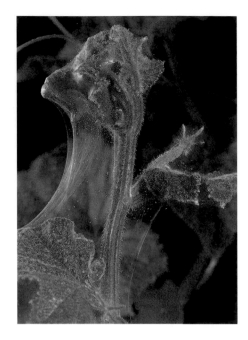

Vine weevils feed on many plants, especially those in containers and under glass, so conservatory climbers can be a prime target. The flightless adult beetles, all of which are female and capable of laying eggs, climb up plants and their supports at night to feed on the leaves, producing notches in the leaf margins as they do so. They are slow moving and will stay still when alarmed, making them an easy target for a nocturnal patrol by torchlight.

The serious damage, however, is caused by their underground larvae – up to 1cm (½in) long grubs, and creamy white with tan-coloured heads – which are voracious and will feed on roots until sometimes whole plants collapse. When buying plants in containers you should always check the roots for any sign of this pest. Treating the roots of container-grown ornamentals with a drench of imidacloprid will control the grubs. Alternatively, use a biological control based on a nematode that infects the larvae. Millions of nematodes are watered into the soil or compost, resulting in whole populations of vine weevil grubs eventually dying out. There are also composts containing imidachloprid to control vine weevil grubs and these can be used when potting plants.

LEFT TO RIGHT: Vine weevil, Clematis wilt and spiider mite damage.

Red spider mites flourish in dry conditions, especially in a hot greenhouse in summer, when they will cause leaf mottling and eventually produce a fine webbing around susceptible plants. Most conservatory plants are at risk from these pests. These are not the blood-red spiders that are seen scurrying around walls and bricks, but much smaller creatures that are barely visible to the naked eye – a magnifying glass will reveal them, sucking the sap on the lower surface of leaves. They are yellowish-green for most of the year, only becoming reddish-orange in the autumn. Since they thrive in hot dry conditions, regular misting in summer and warmer temperatures with plain water can keep their numbers down to manageable levels. There is also an effective biological control, a predator mite that is released into conservatories or greenhouses to feed on the pest. For this predator to be effective there must be no trace of insecticide on the plants, and day temperatures need to be around 20°C (70°F) or more. Badly infested plants should be thrown away and not put on a compost heap.

Distorted leaves and spindly tree and shrub growth can result from spray damage. If you do use chemicals, follow the manufacturer's instructions and only spray on calm, overcast days.

Trees and shrubs

Most trees and shrubs spend their lives growing healthily, and are able to tolerate pests and diseases. As happens elsewhere, it is usually sickly specimens – those under stress from lack of water or nutrients – that fall foul of common ailments.

Canker is a broad term for a patch of dead or dying tissue, caused by fungi or bacteria entering the plant through a wound, most commonly on fruit trees. Cankers start their destructive life at the point where branches have been badly pruned or torn from trees. The cracked, sunken lesions on affected branches and trunks can be cut away and burnt. Take care when pruning or hoeing around plants, and always use clean sharp secateurs and loppers to avoid spreading canker between trees or causing ugly wounds in the first place.

Dieback can affect most trees or shrubs. It starts at the tips of branches, with leaves progressively dying as the problem travels towards the main stem. Possible causes are many: the plant may be short of water, deficient in nutrients, suffering from root disease or have the beginnings of canker. Cut out and burn the affected branch or shoot to halt the spread of the dieback.

'Cuckoo spit' is common on many shrubs in early summer, and is a froth produced by a froghopper, a small cream-coloured sap-sucking insect that hides inside from predators. The froth does no harm to plants and the insect itself causes negligible damage. If the cuckoo spit is disfiguring, you can easily rub it off shoots or blast it away with a hosepipe.

Honey fungus is a serious problem that can affect many trees and shrubs. There are several types, some species are aggressive and kill their hosts quickly, while others grow on dead wood. The first sign of attack is often a general deterioration in the appearance of the plant, sometimes with wilting and dieback. If you suspect honey fungus, scrape away the soil from around a large root or the base of a tree, and peel back some of the outer tissues: white honey fungus mycelium will be sandwiched between the bark and the wood. You may also find black 'bootlaces' (another name for the organism is bootlace fungus) – these are called rhizomorphs and are responsible for spreading the fungus through the soil to healthy roots. The honey-coloured toadstools, its fruiting bodies, usually appear in autumn. Dig up infected plants, removing as much of the root system as possible, and keep an eye on neighbouring woody plants during the following years. Some trees and shrubs are resistant to attack, while others vary in their susceptibility.

Silver leaf is a fungal disease that can affect many plants, particularly plums and flowering cherries. The fungus enters through a wound, spreading through the wood and causing a distinctive silvering on the upper surface of leaves. At the first sign of silvering, prune out the affected part and continue cutting until you cannot see any of the telltale brown stain on the inner plant tissue. This will stop the spread of the disease. You can prevent silver leaf appearing by only pruning cherries and other stone-fruiting trees between early spring and late summer, while they are actively growing. Wounds heal much faster during these months, reducing exposure to the fungal spores.

Dealing with slugs and snails

Alison Mundie, Trials Officer at Harlow Carr, has the task of organizing and maintaining the trial gardens. She grows new plant varieties under normal garden conditions to see how they really perform.

Slugs and snails are the bane of most gardeners' lives, and the subject of many mythical or exotic remedies and preventive treatments. The mild wet climate we have in Britain is ideal for these slippery pests, and moist clay soils can worsen the problem. The Royal Horticultural Society gardens at Harlow Carr has very heavy clay, which you might expect to be a breeding ground for slugs and snails, but care, and the help of local wildlife, means a walk round the gardens reveals a different picture.

Alison Mundie is inspired by people's enthusiasm when they realize they could succeed with their plants despite the apparent problems. She believes that 'integrated pest management is the key' as is looking at the garden as a whole. Here are a few of her tips and ideas on dealing with slugs and snails.

Tips from Harlow Carr

- Use resistant plant varieties wherever possible, and explore alternatives, for example, red, crinkly lettuce leaves are slightly bitter and less attractive to slugs and snails than soft green varieties.
- Harden off tender plants thoroughly before planting them out, because soft lush growth is more vulnerable and a real lure for the pests.
- Think of your garden as a food chain. Slugs and snails do play a part in feeding wildlife.

- Take positive steps to encourage natural predators into the garden. Toads and frogs feed voraciously on slugs, while thrushes concentrate on snails, smashing them on strategically placed stones.
- Relax. Admit that a garden free from slugs and snails is impossible, and can be undesirable.

Effective methods for slug control

There are many different ways of controlling slugs, and no one method has yet appeared to be foolproof. So choose your control strategy.

Barriers are a simple and effective way of protecting plants. Providing an obstacle course of uncomfortable materials can often discourage them from reaching your prized plant (see step 1).

Identify and understand the enemy's behaviour. Slugs and snails usually come out to feed at night. Long, black garden slugs are the most obvious, leaving a silvery mucilaginous trial, and snails crunch underfoot on a damp evening. Keel slugs are more cunning and remain below ground, so they are rarely noticed until plants are damaged.

Clear away potential hiding places, such as piles of leaves in shady corners – remove them to a compost heap or dig them back into the soil. Any other rotting vegetation needs removing as it will attract them and provide perfect breeding grounds.

Tackling slugs and snails

1 Rings of sharp grit around plants lacerate the soft underbellies of slugs and snails. Broken eggshells also work, especially if mixed with dry bran, which absorbs the moisture they need for mobility. Renew when barriers become scattered.

2 Sink special traps or any plastic container into the soil near vulnerable plants, with its rim 2.5cm (1in) above the surface and fill with beer. A morning inspection could reveal many victims. Renew traps every week.

Arm yourself with a torch, a bucket of salted water and gloves and physically remove the pests. Check plants while the slugs and snails are feeding – remember to look underneath leaves, a favourite site. Pick the creatures off and drop them in the salty water, which is lethal to them. Once dead, drain the water and empty them on the compost heap. Don't throw live slugs and snails over the fence: they will find their way back. Continue the nightly patrols regularly, especially after rain.

Biological control is an environmentally friendly way of dealing with surface and underground slugs. It uses a microscopic predatory nematode (*Phasmarhabditis hermaphrodita*) that penetrates their skin and multiplies, preventing them from feeding and killing them. This method is effective for at least 8 weeks before needing a further application and does not taint edible crops, which can be eaten immediately after treatment. However, nematodes do not control snails, are not effective on very clayey soils, and are only active within between 5–20°C (41–68°F). To introduce nematodes, keep them dormant in their carrier powder in the fridge until conditions are right; then mix with water, stir well, and apply the solution to the soil.

Slug pellets should be a last resort in any garden. They are made from bran laced with methiocarb or metaldehyde, which efficiently attracts and poisons slugs and snails. Unfortunately birds, toads, frogs and hedgehogs tend to eat the corpses, and ingest and store the poisons in their own bodies. Use pellets sparingly.

RHS KNOW-HOW

- Grow early potatoes such as 'Kestrel', to harvest before slug populations increase.
- Slug and snail eggs are small white spheres, usually in clusters. If worked to the soil surface, they will be eaten by predators or die in the sun, so keep hoeing.
- Beer traps really do work – and adding grape juice increases the smell and attracts more slugs and snails.
- Plant sacrificial crops near more desirable plants. Slugs and snails always go for the easy target, and may ignore the crops you really want to save and harvest.
- If you use pellets, always protect innocent wildlife by placing pellets under covers raised a fraction at one side to allow slugs and snails access.

INDEX

PICTURE CREDITS

BBC Worldwide would like to thank the photographers below for providing photographs and for permission to reproduce copyright material. While every effort has been made to trace and acknowledge all copyright holders, we would like to apologize should there have been any errors or omissions.

© Jonathan Buckley 4 l & cr, 5 cl & r, 9, 15, 21 l & r, 25, 29, 33 l, 34, 55, 57, 83, 87, 97, 110-11, 112 b, 113, 126, 127, 130, 134, 141, 144, 145, 146 c & r; © Garden Matters 22-23, 33 c, 66 l & c, 81 l & r, 116, 122, 162 c; GPL/David Askham 72, Philippe Bonduel 114, Erika Craddock 98, Claire Davies 21 c, John Glover 28, 60, 75, 91, Neil Holmes 107, 123 l & r, 153 r, Michael Howes 4 r, 59, 81 c, Mayer/Le Scanff 66 r, Clive Nichols 121, 123 c, Howard Rice 13, 26 r, 41, 109 l & c, 118, 125, JS Sira 109 r, Janet Sorrell 120, 151 l, Brigitte Thomas 104, Didier Wallery 14; © John Glover 4 cl, 5 cr, 28, 31, 42 c & r, 45, 46, 47, 53, 88-89, 90, 91, 92 l, c & r, 128-9, 136 b, 149, 157; © Jerry Harpur 69, 155 l; © Marcus Harpur 2, 51, 146 l; © Holt Studios/Phil McLean 99, Nigel Cattlin 151c, 153 l & c, 159 l, 162 l & r, Bob Gibbons 159 r; Andrew Lawson 7, 12, 26 l, 100-1; Matthew Light 164; © Marianne Majerus 20, 26 c, 65, 77, 143, 160; Alison Mundie 56; © Clive Nichols 3, 42 l, 132; © Premaphotos Wildlife/Ken Preston-Mafham 155 c & r; Stephen Record 16; Tim Sandall/The Garden 38, 84, 94 b, 112 t; Mike Sleigh 70; © Derek St Romaine Photography 8, 11, 17, 44, 49, 54, 60-61, 64, 79, 151 r; Janet Uttley 50, 136 t; © Jo Whitworth 5 l, 19, 33 r, 62, 74, 86, 105, 133, 152; © Rob Whitworth 58, 148; Allison Williams 94 t.

USEFUL ADDRESSES

RHS Garden Wisley
Woking, Surrey GU23 6QB
Tel: (01483) 224234

RHS Garden Rosemoor
Great Torrington,
North Devon EX38 8PH
Tel: (01805) 624067

RHS Garden Hyde Hall
Buckhatch Lane, Rettendon,
Chelmsford, Essex CM3 8ET
Tel: (01245) 400256

RHS Garden Harlow Carr
Crag Lane, Harrogate,
North Yorkshire HG3 1QB
Tel: (01423) 565418

For further enquiries and to join the RHS contact: The Membership Dept, Royal Horticultural Society, PO Box 313, London SW1P 2PE
Tel: 0845 130 4646
or visit www.rhs.org.uk